Effective Literature Searching for Research

Second Edition

Sarah Gash

Gower

First edition published 1989 by Gower Publishing Company Ltd.

This edition published by
Gower Publishing Limited
Gower House
Croft Road
Aldershot
Hampshire GU11 3HR
England

Gower
Old Post Road
Brookfield
Vermont 05036
USA

Sarah Gash has asserted her right under the Copyright, Designs and Patents Act 1988 to be identified as the author of this work.

British Library Cataloguing in Publication Data
Gash, Sarah, 1946–
   Effective literature searching for research. – 2nd ed.
   1. Searching, Bibliographical   2. Library orientation
   3. Information resources   4. Learning and scholarship –
   Research   5. Study skills
   I. Title
   025.5´6

ISBN 0-566-08277-2 Hardback
      0-566-08125-3 Paperback

Library of Congress Cataloging-in-Publication Data
Gash, Sarah, 1946–
   Effective literature searching for research / Sarah Gash. – 2nd ed.
        p.   cm.
   Includes bibliographical references and index.
   Rev. ed. of: Effective literature searching for students. 1989.
   ISBN 0-566-08277-2. – ISBN 0-566-08125-3 (pbk.)
   1. Library research–Great Britain.   2. Searching.
Bibliographical.   3. Report writing.   I. Gash, Sarah, 1946–
Effective literature searching for students.   II. Title.
Z710.G25   1999
020´.7´2041—dc21   99-38626
                                                                  CIP

Typeset in Palatino by IML Typographers, Chester and printed in Great Britain at the University Press, Cambridge

Contents

Preface to first edition

I have spent some 15 years working in academic libraries with students and staff from all academic disciplines. Subsequently I have spent a number of years teaching undergraduate and post-graduate students. This experience has enabled me to become familiar with many of the problems encountered by students and other researchers who need to search the published literature in some depth in order to prepare a dissertation, thesis or other research paper. This book is the result.

Using the literature to support research involves much more than a literature search. The thought and preparation beforehand is very important and requires a knowledge of the structure of the literature. The problems of obtaining, recording, reading and citing the literature can be as daunting as the search itself. These topics seem to be somewhat neglected by the literature on infor-mation skills and by the user education programmes given in academic libraries.

This book attempts to explain, in a straightforward manner, techniques, procedures and methods of organization that will enable the reader to understand the environment within which he or she is working and thereby to exploit it more efficiently. It also attempts to dispel some of the mystique which surrounds our library systems and which prevents many people from becoming comfortable with them. Finally it offers some simple guidelines for searching, recording and citing references.

A final word to the reader. Libraries exist to serve the reader. Unfortunately, libraries exhibit a growing tendency to become obsessed with the development and contemplation of more and more complicated systems, many of which are distinctly user-unfriendly. Try not to become intimidated – either by the systems or the librarians. Remember, if it was not for you, both would be out of a job!

Preface to second edition

When I came to update this book, two things struck me very forcibly. One was how much the use of electronic sources had grown in the last ten years. CD-ROM and full text online versions of formerly print-only sources are now commonplace in libraries and, in the former case, also in the home, while the Internet, which was hardly heard of when the first edition came out, is now a major resource to which 20 per cent of the population have easy access. The second point is that, although a researcher must accommodate the new electronic sources in a literature search, these have not replaced, but rather have added to, the traditional print sources. In other words, the job of the searcher has grown and become even more complex than before, but the basic principles are still the same.

This second edition has therefore retained the same structure and much of the original text, which is still completely valid. However, each chapter has required some updating to take account of electronic sources, and all references have been reviewed and updated and quite a number of new ones added. There is also a completely new chapter that considers some aspects of searching the Internet.

The traditional skills of literature searching have not yet

become obsolete. Rather, there is an even greater need to acquire them, though it has to be said that, to many students, this is often more difficult than before. A good searcher needs to have a feel for language and a broad vocabulary and, because many young people are so screen-oriented (both television and computer), the reading of printed text with its wider and more varied vocabulary, and finding the way through the complexities of printed reference works, seems to be quite a struggle. Worse, it is not as cool as surfing the Web, added to which I find that my first-year students have been persuaded by the hype that all the information they will ever need is on the Web. They very soon find that this is far from true, and it is a big shock to them to discover the huge body of academic and other literature in print. Hopefully, this book will assist them to become as effective in using and appreciating the value of printed literature as they do the Internet.

1

Why search?

By *literature search* is meant a systematic and thorough search of all
types of published literature in order to identify as many items as
possible that are relevant to a particular topic. These items could
include not only books, but journal articles, reports, papers given
at conferences or seminars, theses, patents and many other types
of publication. The format of publication is immaterial, as it is the
content that is important to the researcher, and so both printed
and electronic sources – and possibly also audio-visual material
(including microfiche / film) – need to be included in a search.

It is often thought that the only time that people are likely to
need to do an exhaustive literature search is when they are
students. However, the skills of literature searching are the same
as those needed to find any desired information, and the ability to
locate published material quickly and accurately is a skill that will
be useful throughout any person's career. Indeed, an increasing
number of jobs are dealing with exactly this sort of task. Unfortunately, many researchers have had no formal training and so may
not perform at maximum efficiency.

Most students will already have done a certain amount of literature searching in order to find readings that will help in the preparation of essays, reports, seminar papers and other pieces of

coursework demanded by tutors. Very often, however, such searching will not have gone further than using the library catalogue, and the first time that some students may be faced with the necessity of performing a full literature search is when they are required to produce a substantial dissertation in their final year. Other students may arrive at the stage of embarking on a PhD or MSc thesis without ever having had to do such a search or having received any advice or instructions as to how it can best be done. They are then very often at a loss to know how to go about the task and, sad to say, may well not receive any systematic tuition. As a result, it frequently happens that this essential task is neglected or virtually ignored by many students. It is exceedingly unfortunate when this happens because, if the search is not done conscientiously, the quality of the thesis or dissertation will certainly suffer; but there is another even more important consideration.

A thesis, especially a postgraduate thesis, is normally required to be based on original research. If the work presented is found to be a duplication of previously published work (even if unintentional) then it could be invalidated. It is therefore of great importance that the student should, by means of the literature search, have established that the topic being considered for the thesis is truly original. For obvious reasons, this should be done as early as possible.

A lack of knowledge of literature-searching techniques is by no means confined to the student population. Many graduates, once in the workforce, will be involved in research at a higher level, equipped with only rudimentary search skills. It is unfortunately true that there are a surprising number of senior researchers, in industry and commerce and also in the academic world, who have very little idea how to perform a systematic and thorough search and may even be unaware of important sources in their field. In addition, their student experience may have failed to teach them that the literature search is in itself a very important part of the research process, and this is as true in science or technology research as it is for the humanities or social sciences. If a researcher is applying for funding, which these days is much more difficult than before to obtain, it may be crucial to demonstrate in the initial proposal that the proposed project is not duplicating other work either completed or in progress.

In academic research, or work in R & D organizations, apart

from establishing the novelty of a research topic, it is important to have a thorough knowledge of the general subject area within which the specific research topic falls. Such knowledge will not only help to establish the context within which the research will be carried out, but may well also point up questions, anomalies or gaps in existing knowledge that could subsequently be considered as both justification for and an indication of the necessary extent of the research. In other words, a background investigation will help to establish the scope, context and parameters of the research. The identification of the appropriate reading matter will be one result of the literature search and will form the basis of a review of the literature that ought to be an integral part of any research publication.

A further reason – and perhaps the most obvious one – for researching the literature is that it is necessary to unearth all the information that will be used in the research project itself. The researcher will perhaps wish to discuss, theorize, offer opinion, comment and speculation, and even present new information as a result of experimentation or investigation of unpublished or archival material, but none of this can be done in a vacuum. There must be a supporting structure of solid information that has been obtained from the existing literature.

Finally, it is necessary to keep up with the literature that is published during the course of a research project. Many research projects take several years to complete. Others will take less time, but there is bound to be material published as the projects proceed, of which the researchers should be aware. The direction, emphasis or conclusions of the research may require modification to take account of the publication of a new piece of work.

Desk research done in other contexts, for example in a business, a legal office or a management consultancy, is often done for others rather than for the researchers themselves and the information will be treated in a different way. The required end product is the information itself rather than this being used as introductory background or contextual material for an academic or R & D project. However, the process is still very similar to any other literature search as the basic principles are exactly the same regardless of the subject area or the purpose of the search.

It cannot be denied that a really extensive literature search can be a time-consuming business and can appear to be a very complicated and daunting prospect to the inexperienced researcher. However, if the task is tackled systematically and knowledgeably, it should be reasonably straightforward and manageable. Moreover, the information that is the end product of the search should be of high quality, providing a sound basis for the user of the information.

Assistance from the library

Researchers will naturally rely heavily on the library or information centre of their organization, but there are definite limits to the assistance that can be obtained from any one such service. Some users often have rather unrealistic, even unreasonable, expectations, although it should be said that as many others may have little understanding of how much a library can assist them.

A full literature search should not be confined to the material held in one collection. Even a very good library cannot afford to purchase more than a proportion of the publications about a subject and, for a number of years now, most libraries have been subjected to budget restrictions that have severely curtailed their purchasing power. If, therefore, a search is confined to just one collection, the range of items discovered is likely to be at best a restricted, and at worst, a badly distorted and inadequate, representation of what has actually been published. In any case, many industrial and commercial libraries do not hold much material, relying on electronic and other external sources for up-to-the-minute information.

In the academic context, the library is going to be most helpful in the advice that can be given during the search. It is unlikely that academic library staff will be able to do literature searches on behalf of clients (apart from online searches). In any case it is always best for students and academics to do their own searches. As has been pointed out, the search is part of the research process anyway and as such provides a valuable learning experience; further, it is the researcher who will best know whether a reference is really going to be useful. A proxy searcher, however well briefed, cannot have the same perspective on the research project as the researcher. Most academic libraries employ subject specialists, that is, librarians who specialize in a particular subject or group of subjects, often possessing a relevant degree as well as a librarianship or information studies qualification. The staff in industrial, commercial and research libraries are also likely to have an appropriate degree or at least a good deal of practical experience in the subject. Such information professionals can offer invaluable help and advice both before and during the search. Furthermore, they will be in a good position to come across useful material in a serendipitous fashion during the course of their daily routine. It makes good sense therefore for any person involved in a research project to identify the appropriate subject specialist as early as possible and inform him or her about the project. It will be particularly helpful to the librarians if they are given a copy of the search profile (see Chapter 2), which will act as a reminder about the research.

Many academic libraries offer user education programmes that advise students how to exploit the resources within the library. Unfortunately, these are often only arranged for first-year students, well before they need to use the information. Because of this, they may not attend because the relevance and usefulness of the programme is not apparent or, if they do attend, the knowledge obtained may be wholly forgotten by the time the need to use it arises. Other libraries may put on courses especially for students about to tackle a research project. It is worth finding out exactly what is available and, if there is no user education programme arranged, a group of students could perhaps get together and request that one be put on. Alternatively, if there are only one or two students involved, a subject specialist will probably be perfectly willing to provide informal tuition. It is always worth asking. Even if the library is unable to help at all (which is highly unlikely) nothing will have been lost by the enquiry. One word of warning, though. Most user education programmes are based on the facilities actually available in the library and therefore valuable search tools may not be covered because they do not form part of the collection.

Academic libraries also provide a number of printed user guides on various aspects of library use, and these are also valuable as they provide a permanent reminder of what is available and how it can be used. Sometimes these guides are so popular that supplies run out and it is advisable to stock up at the beginning of the academic year when they normally appear in quantity. Similar guides will be found in the larger branches of public libraries.

Industrial, commercial and research libraries are a somewhat different proposition as here a major task of the information professionals employed may be to do searches for the members of the organization and they will probably be experts in the subject. These libraries are anyway less likely to offer user education courses, although many do offer new staff some sort of an introductory tour of, or talk about, the facilities available, perhaps as part of the organization's general induction programme. Even if such an introduction is not offered, the staff will be quite willing to work with researchers on a one-to-one basis, and both parties will benefit from a detailed discussion of the proposed research and a joint planning of the literature search.

Using other libraries

It is always a temptation, because it is less effort, to depend upon the facilities of one library only. This is generally a mistake, for the reasons discussed above. Few libraries have fully comprehensive collections. It is important to identify other potentially useful libraries in the area and further afield. There are a great many very specialized libraries that can supply the detailed information so often required by researchers, but the main problem is to identify what these are. A useful directory to subject collections in the United Kingdom is the *ASLIB Directory* (1), a copy of which will be found in nearly all libraries. A subject librarian will also be able to help in the identification of, and contact with, such libraries, many of which belong to organizations and associations that may be identified in the *Directory of British Associations* (2). Most such libraries will allow outsiders to use their facilities for reference purposes. In the case of research students, it will often be found that neighbouring academic libraries will have arranged reciprocal borrowing rights for each other's members. Even if there is no formal scheme, librarians or academic supervisors will generally be willing to supply students with a letter of introduction which can be submitted to other institutions. Many academic libraries also have schemes whereby individual or organizational clients who are not members of any academic institution may still become members. Details of all such schemes will be available on request.

It is important to observe the proper courtesies when approaching other libraries. A written request should be submitted well in advance, together with the letter of introduction from the home library, or from the academic supervisor in the case of students. Most libraries will co-operate if approached in this manner, even special libraries that are not normally open to the public. However, if someone turns up on the doorstep unannounced and demands access (as not infrequently happens) the reception is likely to be somewhat icy at best or the prospective user may be refused admittance. If it has been necessary to travel a considerable distance to visit the library then everybody's time has been wasted.

Although the assistance provided by libraries is important, the bulk of the work of a literature search will have to be done by the researchers themselves. The most effective search is one that has been carefully considered, properly planned and recorded, and the following chapters offer some discussion of points that should be considered.

References

1. *ASLIB Directory of Information Sources in the United Kingdom.* 10th edn. London, ASLIB, 1998.

2. *Directory of British Associations & Associations in Ireland.* 14th edn. Beckenham, CBD Research, 1998.

2

Preparing the search

Before embarking upon a literature search, it is useful to have as clear an idea as possible of what the scope of the search topic is to be. This may sound obvious but the scope is not always easy to determine. This can be particularly true for students as a dissertation or thesis may be concerned with a process of investigation into a topic that is quite new to them, and they do not have as much subject knowledge and practical experience as an older and more experienced researcher to help them. Therefore, it may not be possible to lay down rigid guidelines right at the beginning. In contrast, researchers employed by an institution may find the parameters of their research strictly controlled for commercial or other reasons. In either case, the results of any literature research will inevitably affect the course and direction of the project to some degree, as facts discovered in the early stages will demand further investigation into matters not previously anticipated. It is always possible, however, to plan some sort of structure for the search and this will make the search process more efficient by giving it direction.

The first task is to become thoroughly conversant with the context of the chosen topic and with the vocabulary used in its discussion. This preparation may involve a good deal of background reading using such sources as subject encyclopedias, textbooks or review articles, as well as discussion with the academic supervisor, project leader or information professional. If this is done thoroughly, the subsequent search will be easier to do because the searcher will be confident with the subject and its vocabulary. Moreover, the material retrieved is likely to be of greater relevance.

During the background reading a list should be compiled of words and phrases which could be used as keywords in the search process. At this stage, as many potential search terms as possible should be collected. Particular care should be taken to list American as well as British terms. In many subjects the difference in terminology may be very marked and it is important to use both versions when using an American index, otherwise much useful material can be overlooked. American spellings, frequently unexpected by the British reader, should also be looked for. There are English-American 'translating' dictionaries that will help with this task, if you can locate them. For example, there is Schur's *English English* (1), which covers differences in grammar and spelling, or Garner's *A Dictionary of Modern American Usage* (2), both of which are American works.

When the initial reading period is completed, it is a good idea to attempt to define the topic in a single sentence – an exercise which concentrates the mind wonderfully. The scope and parameters of the topic should by now be a good deal clearer, so that the literature search may be focused rather than diffuse.

The next step is to answer a series of questions, the most important of which is, 'what types of published materials need to be included in the search to give a complete body of literature on the subject?'. It may be, in an entirely literary topic, for example, that only books are required, but it is more likely that a great range of materials should be included. It is, therefore, worth spending some time in consideration of the characteristics of the major types of literature before deciding what is required. As so much information is now available in more than one format, typically a print and at least one electronic version, the formats available for searching also need to be investigated.

Books

Books are usually the first form of literature to which people will turn for information, no doubt because it is the most familiar. Although for many subjects books will undoubtedly form the major source of information, in as many others they will be of relatively little importance. It is as well to consider a few characteristics of books when preparing a search, in order to decide if they are likely to be a fruitful source of the information that is required.

Books generally take a considerable time to write and possibly a further year or two before they are finally published. Therefore, the information in a book is quite likely to be at least three years older than the date of the book itself. This may well be significant in many scientific and technical subjects where the most up-to-date information possible is required. The books in such subjects generally perform the function of a drawing together and a convenient repackaging of information that has already been published elsewhere. In other words, the book is acting as a secondary source rather than a primary source. It has been said, somewhat cynically, that it takes 20 years for a new theory in physics or chemistry to become sufficiently accepted to appear in the textbooks. While no doubt an exaggeration, this comment has a certain amount of truth in it.

In humanities subjects, the pattern of research and publication is quite different to that of the sciences. There is much less pressure to publish speedily and many books in these disciplines are presenting information that has never been previously published. The book gives far greater scope than other formats for the discussion, analysis, criticism and opinion that are among the features of research in the humanities. Another feature of this area is that older materials are valuable sources and will always remain so. This means that retrospective searching assumes great significance.

The social sciences show a pattern of publication that partakes somewhat of the nature of both the sciences and the humanities. Much original material is published in book form, but there is also a greater amount of journal literature than there is in the humanities and many books are simply drawing this material together.

These comments do no more than offer a brief summary of the main characteristics of scholarly publication in three important branches of knowledge. The whole subject is large and complex and this discussion is only intended to act as a reminder that some thought should be given to the type of material required as well as to the content, as the two factors are to a certain extent interdependent. One of the functions of the background reading that is done for any research project is to develop a feel for the literature of the topic in this respect.

It is a mistake, when searching for books, to expect to find titles that encapsulate the exact subject of the search. If the topic is a very narrow one then it may well not warrant a whole book to itself or there may be just one or two available. Then again, if the idea for the project is really novel there may be no specific titles at all. However, the subject may well have been dealt with as part of a book. In order to discover if this is so, likely titles (usually concerned with a broader subject coverage) have to be identified, obtained and scanned.

There are, of course, many different types of book, each of which has a specific function and will therefore present a particular type of information or present it in a particular way.

A few of the more common categories of books are given below.

1.   Reference books

These contain a mass of factual information, often presented in tabular or similar format rather than text. They are intended for consultation for specific information and not for continuous reading. Quite a number of reference books are now also available on CD-ROM or an online host and these electronic versions will tend to be more up to date. In a literature search, encyclopedias are useful for background reading and for supplying some starter references, and dictionaries for checking the definition and spelling of search terms. Directories may help to identify organizations or individuals with expertise regarding the chosen topic and/or programmes of research that might be relevant. Directories are particularly useful in business for obtaining basic information about companies, products and personnel.

2. Textbooks

Textbooks are designed to assist those who are studying the subject by presenting a structured and concise instructional package. Typically they will cover the basic principles, facts and theories of the subject and may be expected to include such features as worked examples, exercises, further readings and suggestions for project work. They will tend not to cover very new or controversial material in any depth. Allied with the textbook are other instructional publications such as manuals, programmed texts, workbooks and readers.

3. Treatises

A treatise is a very thorough, detailed (not to say exhaustive) treatment of a particular subject. It frequently consists of several volumes and is systematically arranged in some way appropriate to the subject. Usually the reader is assumed to have some knowledge of the topic already and the level of treatment is advanced. Because of the time needed to produce treatises, the cost of publishing them and the difficulties of revision, they seem to be a diminishing category of publication. The great era for such works was the nineteenth century, and many treatises produced then have never been superseded and are still essential sources of information. A treatise may be expected to have extensive bibliographies, which can assist a literature search considerably.

4. Monographs

These are original works, usually on very specialized topics, written by a specialist for specialists. They may well complement a textbook or treatise by giving a detailed treatment of a narrow field. Some monographs, like treatises, may be quite old yet still be the definitive treatment of a subject merely because the topic has not been followed up by anyone in recent years. It could be a mistake to judge the value of a monograph too hastily by means of date alone. Monographs may also be expected to have extensive bibliographies.

5.   State of the art review

These books will collect and integrate previously published material from various sources and present it as an overview of the current state of the subject. They often comment critically on the material but may be purely descriptive. If well done, they may substitute to a certain extent for the primary literature up to the time of publication. However, it is always dangerous to rely on the opinions or accuracy of others and it should be a rule always to work from the primary sources. This type of work is most useful in helping to identify important primary literature and they will invariably have extensive bibliographies. In many subject areas, such review volumes may be produced on a regular basis and published as a series – for example *Annual Reviews in Plant Physiology*. These are often treated as periodicals by libraries and can therefore be overlooked in the book catalogue. Sometimes these titles do not cover the whole field as represented by their title, but focus on a particular aspect of it, often one that has shown rapid or significant developments. This allows greater depth of treatment.

There are other categories of book, but sufficient has been said to show that books carry out a variety of functions, and that the type of treatment that a subject will receive can be anticipated. This is obviously useful knowledge for a researcher. If a particular treatment is required then certain categories of book can be dismissed from the search and time is saved.

Journal articles

In scientific and technical subjects, where the swift dissemination of information is of paramount importance, the preferred medium of publication is the journal article. It is therefore no surprise that over 80 per cent of journal literature falls within these subject areas. However, any literature search, regardless of subject, should include an investigation of journal or periodical literature. The majority of information published today appears in journals and, because of sheer quantity alone, the importance of this material cannot be overemphasized. Other significant characteristics of this type of publication are as follows:

1. Journals contain the most recent material on a subject. This is because journal issues are usually published far more quickly and frequently than books, though, with prestigious titles in particular, articles may take as long or even longer. Electronic journals are particularly speedy in making material available.
2. Journals are able to publish papers that are too short, too ephemeral, too controversial or too obscure to warrant publication in book form. The commercial success of a journal does not depend on the demand for one paper in one issue. A book must sell on its own merit.
3. The current body of journal literature will give an overview of a subject. Retrospectively, it will enable past trends to be identified and followed.

Taken collectively, journals are not a particularly efficient means of disseminating information. This is partly because of the huge numbers that are published. There are many thousands of journals published worldwide and any one library can only hope to subscribe to a tiny fraction of the total. Even in one small subject area it is unlikely that one library would stock all the relevant titles. Many journals are therefore never seen by potentially interested readers.

Another problem is known as the 'scatter phenomenon'. Although the bulk of the most important articles on a subject will be published in a fairly well-defined group of core journals, it has been discovered that up to 20 per cent of significant material will be scattered among a wide range of journals that may not appear to be likely sources. This often happens as a result of the pressure on academics and research workers to publish. The capacity of the core journals is limited and up to 80 per cent or even more of the articles submitted to the more prestigious of them may be rejected. Even so, there may be a long queue of articles waiting to be published and the delay may be as long as two years. Authors tend therefore to publish where and when they can, so contributing to the scatter phenomenon.

A consequence of these factors is that the searcher may be faced with a few problems if an exhaustive search of journal literature is required. It would be a very dangerous thing, for example, to confine a literature search to the titles held in just one library. The scope of the search would be severely restricted and much valuable information would be missed. There is a temptation also (at least in this country) to confine searches to journals published in the English language, but this, too, is a mistake. Much valuable research is going on all over the world, especially in the sciences and technologies. Fortunately for those with little linguistic ability, there is a well-established translations industry and English versions of foreign journal articles can often be obtained without too much difficulty.

As in the case of books there are many categories of journal, each with its own function. From the searcher's point of view they need only be considered as falling into one of two broad divisions. There are the primary journals, which contain new and original work, and the secondary journals that report, review or comment upon work already published. The division is certainly not as clear cut as this might suggest. There are many journals that perform both functions.

Electronic journals

The area of electronic journals is one that has grown very rapidly over the last three or four years. There are now over 3 000 UK titles alone that are available in electronic form, but it is important to consider the distinction between electronic journals and journals which appear in electronic format. True electronic or digital journals are those that appear *only* in electronic form, generally, but not exclusively, on the Internet or one of the academic networks. This is in contrast to those journals which are produced in print but also wholly or partly in electronic format that may be CD-ROM, traditional online hosts such as Dialog, the Internet or other networks such as SuperJANET. It is important in the case of true electronic journals to be aware that the reliability of the content can be at best variable and at worst dubious. Some of these titles are not moderated and anything contributed will be made available to the users. These need to be treated with caution as the lack of moderation can mean that the quality and reliability of the articles is suspect. Other electronic journals, however, are moderated in the same way as reputable print journals traditionally are.

That is, there is a system by which articles that are submitted for publication are passed to two or more academics who are experts in the field. These referees will comment on the article, recommending, as the case may be, acceptance, rejection or acceptance after certain modifications are made by the author. Such a system upholds academic standards in those journals that conform to it. Otherwise, the decision concerning the publication of an article is solely that of the editor(s) or, in the case of certain electronic journals, not even that, as the authors are able to put up their articles themselves. It is important to know which titles are moderated in some way and which are not.

Journals in electronic format are popular with libraries because they overcome many of the administration problems associated with the print title such as missing or vandalized issues, the need to log in every issue and chase up missing ones, the costs of binding or boxing and the enormous amount of shelf space needed to house them. Some special libraries are keen to become almost wholly electronic, the so-called virtual library or digital library that has dispensed with print collections in favour of databases. Most other libraries will subscribe to a number of CD-ROM titles and increasingly will also offer access to electronic journal libraries that comprise a collection of titles offered within one subscription. Because of the variety of formats available it is easy to overlook some of the titles on offer unless care is taken.

Reports

Characteristically, reports are the products of organizations rather than individuals and are compiled as a result of the efforts of a number of people who may or may not be acknowledged in the final work. Reports are often described as being 'half published' because they are rarely published by a commercial publisher but are issued by the organization responsible for their production, possibly in a very informal manner. Most reports are prepared for a particular and limited readership and the number of copies available may be restricted.

There are many different types of report, each serving different functions. For example, there are research and development reports, technical reports and government reports. The common factor is that they will all report the results of, or the progress of, an investigation, and will usually draw conclusions from the facts presented and make recommendations for future activities or development. Government reports in particular will often deal with a specific event and will contain the evidence of witnesses or experts. The value of reports as a source of information is that they tend to contain very detailed descriptions of the investigation, often with much tabular, graphical and statistical material. Unlike many other research publications, they will also describe unsuccessful features of the investigation and analyse why they were unsuccessful.

As reports are generally written during or immediately after the work that they describe and are released quite quickly, they will often contain material that is the latest obtainable in a particular area. They are, therefore, of particular importance in those areas of research where development is very rapid, for example electronics or information technology. Much report literature is of government origin, either directly or indirectly, in that governments are the largest source of funds for research work. The largest single source of reports is the United States government.

Increasingly, reports of various types are to be found on the Internet. In particular, many government and other official reports may be published through this medium.

Well over 20 per cent of all documents cited today are reports, so they are a source of information that cannot be ignored, as most of this information will not be published in another form. In fact reports are challenging journals as the most prolific form of literature. The largest proportion of reports deals with the sciences and technology, but reports are also a very valuable source of information in the social sciences. Retrospectively, as governments have been producing reports for a long time, they form a valuable source of historical information.

Conference literature

Conferences, seminars, symposia, colloquies and meetings show many similar characteristics and for convenience will be referred to by the generic name of conference. This form of literature is probably the most awkward to identify and locate and there is considerable cynicism as to the value of it. Just as there is a pressure to publish, so there is a pressure on academics particularly to enhance their professional reputation (and also obtain travel grants) by giving papers at conferences. Many universities will only subsidize attendance at a conference if the recipient is giving a paper. This in turn leads to pressure on the organizers of such events to accommodate as many speakers as possible, leading to a reduction in the length and quality of the papers presented.

There is in fact a well-known conference circuit in every subject on which the same faces are seen regularly, and it can be quite difficult for a newcomer to join the clique. It is regrettable but true that many papers given at conferences are of little value, often containing an inferior version of what has already been, or is about to be, published elsewhere. Much of the value of attending conferences comes with the discussions after the papers have been given, and these are seldom recorded, let alone published.

A conference may be published in a variety of formats, such as a bound conference volume, as part of a journal, as a supplement to a journal, as reports, as pre-prints or on the Internet. It is because of this lack of uniformity that much conference literature does not find its way into abstracting and indexing journals. Another problem is that there is often a very long delay between the occasion of the conference and the publication of the proceedings, three or four years being not unusual. It is usually assumed that the full proceedings of a conference will be published, but this is not invariably so. Papers may be read, but not included in the proceedings. Others may be promised and advertised, but never materialize. Still others may be given an abstract only.

Some conferences, therefore, can pose a considerable problem to anyone wishing to include this form of publication in a literature search. However, there are many well-established, regularly occurring conferences sponsored by professional and academic institutions that contain useful information and which do not display the difficulties recounted above. This type of literature should not be omitted from the search, but it is essential to evaluate the material fairly carefully.

Theses

A thesis is a piece of original research that is carried out for the purpose of obtaining a higher degree. Its basic function is as a vehicle that allows the student to demonstrate a grasp of the subject and of the research methodology used. The need for originality in a thesis, together with the fact that there is no co-ordination regarding the subjects chosen, means it is less likely that there will be a coherent coverage of any subject than with other forms of literature.

Theses are not publications in the normal sense of the word. Copies are retained by the university of origin but usually nowhere else. Understandably, there is often a reluctance to loan theses because so few copies are in existence and they cannot be replaced if lost. However, the British Library has established a microfilm collection of British theses that is available for loan. Until recently, it was normal to obtain permission from both the author and the academic institution to read a thesis; however, with the advent of a central collection of microfilm this practice seems to be less usual.

As doctoral theses in particular are required to contain original work they can be important sources of primary material. Approximately two-thirds of all British theses are in science and technology and therefore form a substantial body of literature in these areas. The standard of work is sometimes doubted but as each dissertation is supervised by a specialist in the field and examined by up to six other such specialists before a degree is granted, it can be assumed that a certain minimum quality of work is demonstrated. As possibly half the doctoral dissertations may later be published, albeit in a considerably modified form, they must have some value besides that of a degree-earning exercise. It must be said, however, that there has recently been some very severe criticism in the press of the standards and quality of supervision of dissertations and theses.

Patents

Patents are a very rich source of technical information that is far too often neglected in a literature search. The granting of a patent gives the recipient a legally enforceable monopoly to make, use or sell the invention in the country or countries granting the patent. In return for this protection the patentee is required to disclose full details of the invention including detailed illustrations. Patents are probably the most up-to-date form of technical literature since, by definition, the inventions they protect must be novel and no patentee is going to publish details of the invention elsewhere before patent protection is obtained. In fact, much of the information to be found in patents, possibly over 70 per cent, is never published in any other form. The sorts of invention that can be patented include machines, manufactured articles of all kinds and processes or methods of manufacture.

The patent system is designed to encourage industrial development by providing information that can be used to stimulate new ideas and new research while protecting the rights of the inventor. The patents literature is important because:

- it discloses technical information far earlier than any other form of literature;
- it gives very detailed, not to say exhaustive, information including illustrative material;
- it reviews the state of the art leading up to the invention being patented;
- taken collectively, it indicates the current trends of research and, because very few inventions are not given patent protection as soon as possible, patents are a comprehensive and complete body of literature in this respect;
- in retrospect, it provides a record of progress in industry.

Patents are therefore an extremely valuable source of technical information, and no literature search in the area of applied science or technology is complete unless patent literature has been taken into account.

Standards

British Standards are technical agreements published by the

British Standards Institution. They describe how products should be manufactured so that they are fit for the purpose for which they are intended. Standards deal with criteria such as quality, dimensions, testing, terminology and codes of practice for the installation, maintenance and operation of equipment. Most British Standards are recommendations only but some are backed by law, especially those that deal with safety. It is a strong selling point if products conform to British Standards and, therefore, the information that they contain is very important to anyone carrying out research in industry.

The sort of information contained in a British Standard will vary according to the function it is intended to serve, but will include such things as a definition of the topic, the scope and the conditions or applications in which the standard should be used, and the requirements of the standard. Many standards describe test methods and equipment, tables of data and definition of terms. Cross-references to other standards are common.

Although there are a few bodies in Britain that produce their own standards, most work through the national institution. Some countries, such as the United States, differ from Britain in having a very large number of institutions that produce nationally accepted standards. Other countries do not publish standards at all, although all the major industrialized nations do so. The International Standards Organization attempts to develop a system of international standardization and for many British Standards there is a corresponding ISO standard, though the two may not be identical. For the development of any product that is to be exported to another country, the identification of required standards is an essential part of the development process.

Official publications

This term includes government publications and publications of international bodies such as UNESCO, the Food and Agriculture Organization (FAO) or the European Union. Many official publications contain information not found elsewhere and are therefore extremely important sources. Unfortunately, they are also extremely numerous and their organization is a nightmare for those unaccustomed to the bibliographic intricacies of this type of literature. The only common feature of official publications is their diversity in form, in subject and in level of treatment. As governments are involved with most areas of society, this is inevitably reflected in the publications and there are very few subjects that are not covered. However, topics such as science and technology, medicine, agriculture and allied industries, social sciences and education probably predominate, together of course with legislative material and statistics of which governments are the most prolific producers.

Format is equally diverse. Reports predominate, but monographs, pamphlets, reference books, manuals and journals will all be found along with parliamentary papers, bills, acts, and so forth. Many official publications are published in an electronic format as well as in print. Level of treatment is equally diverse and ranges from that suitable for primary school to advanced research material. Most people will have used official publications, but very often their origin is not recognized. Searchers of the literature, be they interested in history, politics, economics, science, technology or many other subjects, should consider carefully the extent to which this type of material should feature in the search.

Other search parameters

The decision as to which types of materials are required for the research in hand is fundamental to literature search, as this will determine the sources that need to be searched. However, there are other parameters that should also be considered before the search starts.

Date

What is the earliest date of publication that is acceptable and what is the latest? Date of publication should not be confused with a period within the topic. For example, a historical thesis may be concerned with events between 1882 and 1901 but the earliest useful date might be 1870, because factors leading up to the period under consideration must be considered. There may not be a cut-off date, as material on this period might continue to be published to the present day, but the scope of the thesis could suggest that material published after, for instance, 1914 is not required.

Language

If material is found that is in a foreign language, is it to be followed up? Most researchers can cope with one or perhaps two languages in their own subject but other material may be unusable unless a translation is found or commissioned. The difficulty here, of course, is that such material may be extremely important and its omission undesirable. The problem must be carefully considered for every search. If it is likely that translations will have to be commissioned then funds will need to be found for this purpose. Some libraries (including the British Library Document Supply Centre at Boston Spa) will arrange this for clients and may bear the cost themselves. It is a good idea to find out what facilities are available as soon as it appears that they will be needed, as the delay can be considerable.

Country of origin

This factor is linked with language to a certain extent, but there are many non-English-speaking countries that publish largely or exclusively in English because it is the major academic international language. The origin of the material may, however, be important, as for example with topics dealing with educational, social or legislative systems. However, there is nothing to stop an American from writing about any aspect of British life or vice versa. There is often a problem in sifting out British material from an American source, especially in a manual search, as the country of origin generally does not feature in printed indexes. A decision must be made concerning the importance of this factor. It may be desirable to confine a search to sources produced in this country.

SEARCH PROFILE

Title:

> Investigation of the incorporation of teaching of personal skills in higher education courses in the U.K.

Scope of search:

> All subjects taught at H. E. level. Interested in depts teaching rather than centralised units such as an E. D. U. but include latter at least at first.
> Exclude: Colleges of F. E.
> Study / learning skills, teaching outside H. E. context.

Parameters:

> Date: 1970 — to date.   Current position of greatest interest.
> Languages: English — unlikely to find in other languages
> Country: U.K. (Lots of U.S. material published.
> Format: Any. Most likely to be j. articles, reports, conference lit. & official publs.

Key words:

> Personal skills, transferable skills, verbal skills
> "   capabilities   communication skills
> "   competencies   writing skills

Known references:

> GASH, S. & REARDON, D.F. Personal transferable skills for the modern information professional. J. Information Science, Oct. 1988.

Figure 2.1   Example of a search profile

Search profile

When all these points have been considered and the parameters of the search are set, a search profile should be written (see Figure 2.1 on p. 25). This is simply a record of the parameters which can be used to ensure consistency in the search. Copies can also be given to the specialist librarian to act as a reminder of the research project. It is very likely that the search profile will be modified in response to the results from the initial stages of the search, and there is nothing wrong in this. However, it is useful to have some guidelines to work to initially as they help to focus the search. It is very easy to become sidetracked during a literature search and if this happens a good deal of time can be wasted. The profile, if frequently referred to, will prevent this, and it can be modified if and when necessary.

References

---

1.   SCHUR, N.W., *English English*. 2nd edn. Essex Conn., Verbatim, 1980.

2.   GARNER, B.A., *A Dictionary of Modern American Usage*. New York, Oxford University Press, 1999.

3

Sources and tools

When the searcher has a clear idea of the scope of the subject of the search and of the type of materials that are required, the search may begin. The stages of a systematic literature search are generally carried out in a particular sequence, which is the one advocated here. There are practical advantages in keeping to this sequence. For one thing, it begins with the easier and probably more fruitful tasks and moves on to the more awkward stages, by which time the novice searcher will have gained useful experience in handling bibliographic tools of all sorts. Another advantage is that the earlier work may well provide information that will lead into and support the later stages of the search. It may be, of course, that the parameters of a particular search will make certain stages redundant. A thesis that is based on eighteenth-century literary texts, for example, may require only books and journal articles. In such cases the sequence of search must be modified to match the requirements.

In discussing the sequence of search it is not possible for a work of this scope to list all the individual titles that could be searched. The emphasis will therefore be on *types* of source with some indicative titles for English language publications. The organization of literature is such that these types of publication will have equivalents in every subject and in many countries of the world. Providing the searcher knows the type of source that is required, it is easy to discover the precise title. For example, enquiries as to the existence of a national bibliography of Singapore or a listing of the national standards of France will lead to the identification of the Singapore National Bibliography or the Catalogue des Normes Françaises. Actually getting hold of copies of these to search may be more difficult, of course, and this problem is discussed in Chapter 7.

The first step, then, is to identify and list the sources that are to be used in the search and there are many tools that will assist in this work.

Guides to the literature

One of the most useful tools for a novice searcher to identify is a guide to the literature of the subject within which the search topic lies. There have been several series produced, such as the Pergamon *'How to find out about...'* and the Bowker-Saur *'Information sources in...'* series. Numerous other publications with titles such as 'Guide to the literature of...' or 'Guide to information sources in...' have been produced by a number of publishers in the past and cover a wide variety of subjects. They may be traced by title or subject in library catalogues, or by title in *Whitaker's Books in Print* (1), or the subject specialist in a library should be able to identify the appropriate works. Some of these guides may be somewhat out of date but the major reference tools probably have changed little, if at all, and therefore these works are still very valuable. They will deal in depth with all types of material relevant to the subject and list the specialist sources. It is worth purchasing such a guide if it is in print.

Two other more general guides to reference tools are Walford's *Guide to Reference Material* (2) and Balay's *Guide to Reference Books* (3). Both are multi-volume works that have an international coverage, but Walford has a British and Balay an American emphasis. All major subject areas are covered in both works, and they are invaluable tools to any researcher as they list all the major reference works for each topic.

Stages of the search

Stage 1

Source to search — Library catalogue
Document type retrieved — Mostly books, but also pamphlets,
reports, conferences, audio-visual
material, etc.

In order to get the most out of the library catalogue it is necessary
to understand the general principles of library arrangement. It
may be a very pleasant activity, as well as occasionally rewarding,
to browse along the shelves, but it should be remembered that the
material available represents what has been left behind by other,
presumably discriminating, readers. The most useful items may
well be on loan, in use, or waiting to be reshelved. The fact that
many libraries have separate shelf sequences for oversized books,
reference material, short loan items, and so on, is also easily overlooked. The only complete list of what is available in a library is
the catalogue.

Most academic libraries will use one of the major classification
schemes – Dewey Decimal, Universal Decimal (UDC) or Library
of Congress – or a variation thereof. Libraries of specialized institutions may use schemes that have been developed specifically for
the subject area of interest. The catalogue may be in the form of
microfiche or more likely a computer database accessed by terminals in the library and increasingly, as institutions become networked, in the office. However, whatever the scheme and
whatever the form the general principles are the same in each
library.

Theoretically, a classification scheme is devised so that material
on any one subject will be found at only one shelf number (sometimes referred to as the call number). In practice, however, it is not
possible to place all related material together because most subjects can be approached from a great many angles – historical,
cultural, sociological – or are by nature interdisciplinary, such as
medical physics or social psychology. Any boundaries that are
drawn must of necessity be somewhat artificial. A book will therefore be given a shelf number that reflects the aspect of the subject

that is given greatest emphasis by the author or that is of greatest interest to that particular library. If it treats a number of aspects with equal emphasis (for example, a physics textbook may cover heat, light, magnetism and electricity), then it will be placed at a general number even though it contains very specific material. The shelf number is really only a finding device that indicates the physical location of an item. It may include not only a subject classification but also coded indication of such things as author, size, special collections, availability for loan, and so on. A book will be given only one shelf number.

Whereas a book will only appear at one place on the shelves, it can appear in several places in the catalogue, which is a very flexible tool. If the title reflects several aspects of a subject, each of which has a specific number in the classification scheme being used, then it can be given several 'added' classification numbers and have an entry under each of these in the classified catalogue. This allows searchers to find relevant material that could otherwise be missed.

British libraries, and especially academic libraries, tend to favour the classified approach, which means that they will provide a name catalogue, which is an alphabetical sequence of authors and titles; a classified catalogue, which is a numerical or alphanumerical sequence of classification numbers; and an alphabetical subject index. In order to carry out a subject search it is necessary first to consult the subject index under all possible keywords and make a list of all the corresponding classification numbers. These numbers should then be looked up in the classified sequence of the catalogue and the full range of relevant items will be displayed, regardless of where they are actually shelved. The temptation to go directly to the shelves from the subject index in order to browse should be firmly resisted for the reasons given above.

Many public libraries and most libraries in the United States prefer the dictionary catalogue approach. The dictionary catalogue provides a single alphabetical sequence of authors' names, titles and subject terms under which relevant titles are listed. Readers often find this an easier system to understand but it can be tedious and frustrating to use for an exhaustive search, as one is constantly being referred to different parts of the catalogue. This is because the terminology of one coherent subject may be very diverse alphabetically. The dictionary catalogue is never as precise a system as a classified catalogue and, if poorly constructed, can be almost useless.

Whichever system is used in a particular library, it is important to understand the principle of how it works in order to get the most out of it in a literature search. Most libraries will have leaflets explaining the use of the catalogues and these should be collected and studied carefully. It is also useful to get hold of a copy of the classification scheme itself and find out how it treats the topic of the search.

Stage 2

Source to search	–	Book bibliographies
Document type retrieved	–	Books, occasionally reports, conference proceedings and other monographic publications.

The word bibliography in this context means an organized list of books. The task of compiling bibliographies is a very important one, the more so because of the enormous growth in book publishing since the war. Without this type of tool it would be impossible to keep track of what is being published. The ultimate in bibliographies would be a single list of all books published in all countries. With recent developments in computer technology this would not be an impossible task, but such a universal bibliography seems destined to remain a theoretical rather than a practical concept. Book bibliographies that are available to most searchers fall into four important groups.

National bibliographies
These are produced by nearly all countries with any sort of publishing activity. The principle behind any such bibliography, as its name suggests, is that it should be a regularly issued ongoing publication that lists all books that are published within a particular country. In fact, the scope of national bibliographies does vary somewhat from country to country. The French like to include everything published in French regardless of origin, whereas the Australians try to include everything written by Australians or about Australia, again regardless of where it was actually

published. Each publication will indicate the scope of the work and it is as well to check both what is included and what is omitted, as there is no true standardization between countries. Particulars of all the national bibliographies that are currently produced may be found in UNESCO's *Bibliographical Services Throughout the World* (4).

Nearly all national bibliographies will allow access by subject. The weekly *British National Bibliography* (5) is arranged by Dewey classification number, which allows easy searching. The United States, oddly enough, does not have an official national bibliography, but a title that is widely used as an equivalent in this country is the monthly *Cumulative Book Index* (6). This reflects national preference in being arranged in a single sequence like a dictionary catalogue. Both these titles produce regular cumulative indexes, not just annually but every three or five years as well, and this is very economical of time when searching retrospectively. National bibliographies are useful for both current and retrospective searching, and as both these titles are widely found as the CD-ROM version and are also available online, this can be done very easily.

Trade bibliographies
For current information, the bibliographies produced primarily for the book trade are useful and these are generally to be found in academic libraries and larger branches of public libraries. Sometimes they may not be put out on the shelves but are retained in the librarians' workrooms. However, readers will almost certainly be allowed access on request. The two bibliographies that give an indication of whether titles are actually in print and therefore purchasable are the previously mentioned *Whitaker's Books in Print* (1) for the UK and the American equivalent *Books in Print* (7), with which it is often confused because of the similarity of name. They are, however, completely different publications. If it is important to keep abreast of the current book literature, sources that list books published within the last few weeks and to be published in the near future include, for Britain, *The Bookseller* (8), which is weekly, and for the United States, the *American Book Publishing Record* (9), which is monthly. Both provide subject listings, which are useful features for the searcher.

Library catalogues
Many large or specialist libraries have in the past published their catalogues and these can be useful for searching for older material. Owing to the high cost of subscribing to some of the major tools in this category, however, they are likely to be found only in larger and comparatively richer libraries. The *British Library General Catalogue* (10), formerly the *British Museum Catalogue*, is a valuable publication, as is the American equivalent, the enormous *National Union Catalog* (11), produced by the Library of Congress. Unfortunately the sheer size of this latter publication is extremely daunting to the user and for both titles the subject indexes are somewhat limited and can be difficult to use. More accessible, and in most cases easier to search, are the many catalogues of (mostly) academic libraries that may be accessed electronically via JANET (Joint Academic NETwork). This is an extensive system linking UK academic libraries, research councils and the British Library and allows the user to log on to individual library catalogues and search interactively.

Specialist subject bibliographies
The tools so far mentioned are general in that they cover all subjects. It would be particularly useful if the searcher could discover an up-to-date specialist bibliography that covers the topic in hand. There are thousands of such subject bibliographies and suitable titles may well be discovered while searching the general categories of book bibliographies considered above, but there are also some bibliographies of bibliographies that are likely to be more useful. The *Bibliographic Index* (12) is a four-monthly periodical that lists not only bibliographies published in book or pamphlet form but also those published as part of a book or appended to an article in any one of nearly 3 000 journals. It covers the humanities and sciences and is useful as a current source, though there is an American bias.

T. Besterman's *A World Bibliography of Bibliographies* (13) lists in 5 volumes some 117 000 bibliographies by subject and is the most comprehensive tool of this type. It is considerably dated now, having been published in 1965, but is still of value to those serious researchers who wish to find older material, providing they can access a copy. An update for the period was attempted by A.F.Toomey, but this is not so well presented.

Sizeable bibliographies that occur in books may also be located in online book bibliographies as there will be a field in the record in which the item is tagged with the word 'bibliography(ies)'. Once the appropriate field is identified from the database sheet it can be incorporated as part of the search along with the subject keywords. (See Chapter 4 for more information on online searching.)

Stage 3

Source to search   –   Abstracting and indexing journals
Document type retrieved   –   Journal articles, but also reports, conference papers, occasional books and, in science titles, patents and sometimes standards.

Most journals provide contents pages for each issue and also an annual index. However, it is extremely tedious and time-consuming to search journals title by title in this manner, as well as being quite unnecessary. The tools to use are the abstracting and indexing journals, commonly but rather loosely referred to as abstracts and indexes. They both have a similar function, which is to scan a large number of journals within a particular subject area and produce a collective listing of all the articles. Because they are nearly always concerned with the subject rather than with geographical restriction, the scope of most abstracting and indexing journals is worldwide. There are a few, however, that confine themselves to the journal publications of a single country. There are many hundreds of abstracting and indexing tools and there will be very few topics which are not catered for by at least one title and many subjects are covered by several. Any one library will only be able to subscribe to a few of these tools, either print or CD-ROM, and it may well be necessary to use the resources of several libraries for a comprehensive search or to ask for an online search. A huge number of abstracting and indexing journals are to be found on the big supermarket online hosts such as Dialog and Datastar and this is probably the best way to search them. However, many of the small specialist titles are still not available electronically because they are too small to warrant the expense of doing this. Such specialist titles should not be overlooked as they often cover journals that are not otherwise indexed and / or cover very specific subject areas that exactly match the interests of the researcher.

In order to find out what abstracting and indexing journals exist in any field, it will be necessary to consult a directory of periodicals such as *Ulrich's International Periodicals Directory* (14), or a very similar work published by Ebsco entitled *The Serials Directory* (15). Ebsco also publishes the *Index and Abstract Directory* (16), which offers a classified listing and is easier to use.

Abstracting and indexing journals are issued at regular intervals, typically monthly, and are cumulated annually. They are useful, therefore, for both current and retrospective searching. There are three important points to remember when searching these tools. First, a list of search terms should be compiled and all terms should be used when searching. Quite often the indexing terms used will vary slightly from year to year, reflecting the evolving vocabulary of the subject or even an inconsistency in indexing policy. Second, it should be a rule always to start searching the most recent issues and work back. The searcher may be lucky to come across a recent review article with an extensive bibliography that could save a great deal of work. Third, it should be remembered that true electronic journals are generally *not* covered at all by these tools. In fact the bibliographical control of the contents of such journals is currently almost non-existent, which is a considerable problem for any researcher.

Indexing journals
These are the simpler of the two types of tool. Indexing journals are typically arranged in alphabetical order of subject headings. Under each heading are listed the papers pertaining to that subject. The reference is very brief, consisting of the author(s)' name, title of article, title of the journal in which it was published and details of volume, part and page numbers and the year of publication. Some indexes also give an indication of language, whether the article is illustrated and if it has a list of references. A separate author index is usually provided as well, though as with other American titles many use the preferred single sequence of authors, titles and subjects. Indexing journals are very easy to use, as they are arranged in essentially the same way as many familiar reference books such as encyclopedias or British Telecom's

Yellow Pages. However, the information they give is very brief and the searcher is totally dependent on the subject heading used and on the title when deciding whether the article is one that should be read or not. If the title is not an informative one, or the indexing is very general, it can be difficult to judge relevance. The main advantage of indexing journals over abstracting journals is that they can be produced more quickly and are therefore more up to date.

Abstracting journals
These tools differ from the above in the amount of information about each article. In addition to the details given in indexing journals, the reference includes a short summary or abstract of the article. The information in the abstract will obviously give a much better (though not complete) idea of the usefulness of the article and it is therefore much easier to decide if it needs to be read or not. However, because of the time needed to prepare this extra information, abstracting journals tend to be less up to date.

The other major difference is in the arrangement. The entries are arranged primarily by abstract number, although they are often grouped under very broad subject headings. These headings are of little use for a specific search, so it is necessary to use the subject indexes in order to identify relevant references. Under each index term there will be a list of abstract numbers and the searcher must look up each of these in the numerical sequence of abstracts and study the details in order to decide how useful the reference is. It is therefore a somewhat longer process than using indexing journals but has the advantage of providing a more accurate assessment of relevance.

It may well be discovered that there are several abstracting or indexing journals that cover the topic being searched. Although these may overlap to a certain extent, their coverage will be sufficiently different to warrant searching as many of the titles as can be found. Another good reason for comprehensive searching is that some of these tools will index all articles from some journals but only selected articles from others. It is therefore possible for some articles to slip through the net in one case but be picked up elsewhere. A list of the journals scanned by any one title will be published at regular intervals, often in the annual cumulations.

Stage 4

Source to search   – Current Awareness Services
Document type retrieved – Journal articles.

The time lag between an article being published in a journal and being cited in an abstracting or indexing journal may be three to six months or even longer. As an important feature of journal literature is its currency, this delay is obviously detrimental. In order to bridge the gap a number of Current Awareness Services (CAS) are available. The emphasis in these publications is on speed of production rather than sophistication of presentation. A favourite method is to reproduce the contents pages of the journals and present them in alphabetical order of title. The various *Current Contents* (17) titles produced by the Institute of Scientific Information (ISI) are the best-known examples and, though expensive, are taken by many libraries. (Despite the name of the publisher, arts, humanities and social sciences are all covered by this series.) The speed of production is undeniable. In some cases the title page may appear of an issue that has not yet been published and is therefore unobtainable immediately, which can be frustrating. However, the use of these tools is a little tedious as every title page must be scanned. It is also important to be aware that most CAS cover far fewer journals than do the abstracting and indexing services, dealing only with the major titles in each subject. Scanning CAS is therefore not something that can replace the regular searching of the incoming issues of abstracts and indexes. It must be considered as a supplementary activity only.

Stage 5

Source to search   – Special indexes
Document type retrieved – Reports, conferences, theses,
                             patents, standards, official
                             publications.

These categories of material are known to librarians as 'grey literature' as they tend to be less well recorded and somewhat more awkward to search. A number of the traditional abstracting and indexing journals include these materials to some extent, but coverage may be very patchy. It is necessary to check the scope notes of the individual search tools to establish whether any of these types of document are included and, if so, how comprehensive the coverage is. However, for comprehensive coverage, it is necessary to use the special indexes for each category of material.

Reports
The identification and availability of reports is a very 'grey' area, as they are often not published in the strict sense of the word. There are a number of specialized announcement journals that deal solely or largely with report literature, but even these do not show complete coverage.

The largest single collection of reports is held by the British Library Document Supply Centre at Boston Spa and they issue a monthly list entitled *British National Bibliography for Report Literature* (18). This is primarily an accessions list, so detail is sparse and there are no abstracts. Quarterly keyword indexes are produced and there are annual indexes by author, keyword, organization and report number. A characteristic of all reports is that they have a report number which is generally the most important piece of information for subsequent identification of the report and should always be included in the reference. Another useful tool is the *Reports Index* (19), which is available in a variety of formats.

The United States produces a tool that was designed specifically for use by librarians and technical information specialists and is very easy to use. *Government Reports Announcements and Index* (20) is an excellent source of all US government reports and reports that have been sponsored or partially sponsored with US government money, regardless of where in the world the research was carried out. Detail is complete, including an abstract, and the index provides for every possible access point. This work covers all subject areas including the humanities and social sciences, and it is rare to find a subject that is not mentioned – although the emphasis is on science and technology. There is an online version available called *NTIS* which is available on Dialog and Datastar. There are several other US publications, mostly in the hard sciences, that are more specific in coverage, such as *Scientific and Technical Aerospace Reports* (21).

Conferences

If anything, this type of literature is even harder to search because of the variety of methods of publication as discussed in Chapter 2. In the UK it is once again the British Library Document Supply Centre at Boston Spa that holds the largest collection of such material in the country and maintains a comprehensive internal catalogue. The index that is published is *Index of Conference Proceedings Received* (22), which is a very brief accessions list with little detail in the entries.

The United States produces the *Directory of Published Proceedings* (23), an Interdok publication which comes in four series, MLS (Medical and Life Sciences); PCE (Pollution Control and Ecology); SEMT (Sciences, Engineering, Medicine and Technology); and SSH (Social Sciences and Humanities). Much more detail is given in this publication than in the British list. However, none of these lists confines itself to national conference proceedings but all have an international coverage. There may therefore be a certain degree of overlap between the British and American titles.

The titles above record the actual conference, but there are sources that record the individual conference papers, which may be more useful. These are *Conference Papers Index* (24), a bi-monthly published by Cambridge Scientific Abstracts that is cumulated annually, and two titles published by ISI, *Index to Scientific and Technical Proceedings* (25), which is monthly, and its quarterly sister publication, *Index to Social Sciences and Humanities Proceedings* (26). These titles allow access by author/editor, subject, names of organizations and sponsors and even the location of the conference.

There are also sources listing conferences that are planned to be held some time in the future, some titles giving up to two years notice of such events. However, these are outside the scope of this work, which is concerned with sources of published material only.

Theses

Theses for higher degrees are relatively easy to track down. In the United Kingdom the standard reference tools are the previously mentioned *British National Bibliography for Report Literature* (18) from the British Library and the ASLIB publication, *Index to Theses Accepted for Higher Degrees by the Universities of Great Britain and*

Ireland (27), usually referred to more briefly as the ASLIB Index. Details in both of these are rather brief.

The American publisher University Microfilms Inc. produces a work entitled *Dissertation Abstracts International* (28). This contains full details including a comprehensive abstract. The work appears in three sections: A – Humanities and Social Sciences, B – Sciences and Engineering and C – Worldwide. Whereas this tool is very reliable for theses from North America, the Worldwide section (formerly a European section) is not as comprehensive. Most of the titles listed in *Dissertation Abstracts* are available for purchase from the publisher.

Patents

A number of scientific and technical abstracting and indexing journals include patents relevant to their particular subject areas, notably *Chemical Abstracts* (29), which also supplies special patents indexes. However, for a comprehensive search it is necessary to use the indexes published by the patents offices of respective nations. In this country, the Patents Office publishes the weekly *Official Journal (Patents)* (30), which outlines the new applications made and announces imminent publications. It also produces the *Abstracts and Abridgements of Patent Specifications* (31), which is not only published weekly but also in cumulated volumes, which allow easier retrospective searching. Most libraries will not carry these tools and it is necessary either to visit the Patents Library itself, which is housed at the British Library, or one of the regional patents libraries or patent information centres, of which there are some 27 based in major cities throughout the country.

For an international perspective, rather than accessing the various national publications, it is easier to search comprehensive indexes such as the online *World Patents Index* (32), particularly useful for tracing equivalent patents in other countries. Many national and international patents indexes are also available online, some on full text databases. The problem here is that only the text is available, not the diagrams, which are often the most valuable part of the patent in answering queries or solving a problem.

Standards

British Standards are listed in the annual *B.S.I. Standards Catalogue* (33). Although the index is not of the highest quality, it is relatively simple to track down relevant standards. British Standards are also available on a number of CD-ROMs from different producers. Those international standards that have been adopted as British Standards are listed in the BSI catalogue, but the International Standards Organization has its own *I.S.O. Catalogue* (34). There are five types of European standard from different bodies and the easiest method of access is via the *PERINORM* database on CD-ROM produced by Technical Indexes (35), which includes standards from all the national standards authorities in Europe including UK, EU and international standards.

The United States is a more difficult proposition as it has a couple of hundred organizations that produce standards. The American National Standards Institute produces an annual *Catalog* (36), while institutions that publish their own standards will also produce their own lists. For example, the American Society for Testing and Materials publishes the *Annual Book of ASTM Standards* (37). Sources of standards will also be discussed in guides to the literature of science and technology.

Official publications
Because these emanate from a very great number of sources it takes both energy and persistence to carry out a comprehensive search. Identifying and locating the necessary indexes is a considerable task in itself, and if this material is required it is advisable to consult a specialist guide such as D.R. Butcher's *Official Publications in Britain* (38). A common mistake made when searching for British official publications is to assume that they are all or largely published by The Stationery Office (TSO, formerly HMSO), the official government publisher. In fact, TSO publishes only about 30 per cent of the total. These titles are quite easily traced by using the TSO's own lists, especially the *Monthly* (39) and *Annual* (40) catalogues. The *Sectional* lists, which take a departmental or subject approach, show what is actually in print and form a useful source. The most complete single source is *UKOP, the Catalogue of United Kingdom Official Publications* (41), which covers all TSO publications whether or not they are still in print, and all publications from international and European organizations that are distributed by TSO. It also includes all British official publications not published by TSO. For the researcher who requires up-to-the-minute information, the daily lists of TSO publishing can be

consulted on the Internet site (42), which gives all the TSO publications.

The list of non-TSO publications on *UKOP*, produced by individual departments, nationalized industries (those that are still in existence) and numerous bodies in some way linked with government, is provided by a commercial publisher, Chadwyck-Healey. They publish the same information in print as a bi-monthly catalogue with annual cumulations that is entitled *Catalogue of British Official Publications not Published by TSO* (43). They can also supply microfiche copies of most of the items listed.

International bodies which produce official publications often produce their own catalogues and indexes of items that are available. For example, most of the major United Nations agencies do this, such as the International Labour Organization, UNESCO or the World Health Organization.

Statistical sources, both national and international, are often required by researchers. The Office for National Statistics (formerly the Central Statistical Office) has published a *Guide to Official Statistics* (44), which allows subject access and lists the various sources of British statistics in each case. There are also a number of international guides such as the United Nations' *Directory of International Statistics* (45).

Stage 6

Source to search	–	Institutions and people
Document type retrieved	–	Almost anything.

Admittedly not direct sources of printed material, nevertheless, if gaps still remain at the end of a traditional literature search, it is well worth attempting to identify institutions that might be able to help. Contacting libraries which have special collections can be fruitful and they can be identified by using the *ASLIB Directory of Information Sources in the United Kingdom* (46). The identification of professional bodies, societies and associations is also useful. Most of these will have an information service of some sort and may be able to supply bibliographies or put the researcher in contact with some knowledgeable individual. The *Directory of British Associations & Associations in Ireland* (47) is a comprehensive listing of national institutions. Individuals working in the field can also be identified either by retrieving one of their publications or by referring to a register of current research such as *Current Research in Britain* (48).

It should be emphasized that these sources should not be used until all others have been exhausted. Most libraries' information services are willing to help anybody, even if unconnected with the parent organization, in an emergency. However, they do not have the time or the obligation to do work that could quite easily be done by the requester. It should be remembered that one unreasonable person is likely to make a library less sympathetic to the next, possibly well-justified appeal. It is advisable to err on the side of formality in approaching other libraries and institutions, and a formal thank you when help is forthcoming is much appreciated.

References

1. *Whitaker's Books in Print*. London, Whitaker, 1999 (4 vols). (Formerly known as *British Books in Print*.) Annual.

2. WALFORD, A.J., *Guide to Reference Material*. 7th edn. London, Library Association, 1996–98 (3 vols).

3. BALAY, R., *Guide to Reference Books*. 11th edn. Chicago, American Library Association, 1996.

4. UNESCO, *Bibliographical Services Throughout the World*. Paris, UNESCO, 1984. Quinquennial.

5. *British National Bibliography*. London, British Library Bibliographic Services, 1950–. Weekly, with interim and annual cumulations that are also available on microfiche. It is also available on CD-ROM and online.

6. *Cumulative Book Index; a world list of books in the English language*. New York, H.W. Wilson, 1898–. Monthly, except July and August, with quarterly and annual cumulations in print. Also available on CD-ROM, online and on the Web. It is not, despite the sub-title, comprehensive for countries other than the United States, for which it is excellent.

7. *Books in Print, 1998/99* (9 vols). New Providence NJ, Bowker, 1999. Annual but also available online and on CD-ROM.

8. *The Bookseller.* London, J. Whitaker, 1858–. Weekly.

9. *American Book Publishing Record.* New York, Bowker, 1960–. Monthly, with annual and five-year cumulations.

10. *British Library General Catalogue of Printed Books to 1975.* Munich, Saur (360 vols). There are also updating supplements.

11. *National Union Catalog of Books.* Washington, Library of Congress. Monthly, but regularly cumulated.

12. *Bibliographic Index; a subject list of bibliographies in English and foreign languages.* New York, H.W. Wilson, 1937–. Three issues per year, the third cumulating the other two.

13. BESTERMAN, T., *A World Bibliography of Bibliographies and Bibliographical Catalogues, Calendars, Abstracts, Digests, Indexes and the Like.* Lausanne, Societas Bibliographica, 1965–6 (5 vols).

14. *Ulrich's International Periodicals Directory; including irregular serials and annuals.* 36th edn. New York, Bowker, 1998 (5 vols). Annual, also available online.

15. *The Serials Directory, 1986–.* Ipswich, Ebsco. Annual.

16. *Index and Abstract Directory; an international guide to services and serials coverage.* Ipswich, Ebsco, 1989–. Biennial.

17. *Current Contents:*

    ● Agriculture, Biology and Environmental Sciences
    ● Arts and Humanities
    ● Clinical Medicine
    ● Engineering, Computing and Technology
    ● Life Sciences
    ● Physical, Chemical and Earth Sciences
    ● Social and Behavioral Sciences

    Philadelphia, Institute of Scientific Information. All are produced weekly.

18. *British National Bibliography for Report Literature.* Boston Spa, British Library Document Supply Centre, 1998–. (Formerly *British Reports, Translations and Theses.*) Monthly.

19. *Reports Index.* Leatherhead, Langley Associates, 1979–. Also on CD-ROM.

20. *Government Reports Announcements and Index.* Springfield, National Technical Information Service, 1974–. (Formerly issued as two titles, *Government Reports Index* and *Government Reports Announcements.*) Bi-weekly, also online.

21. *STAR; Scientific and Technical Aerospace Reports.* Washington, NASA, 1963–. Semi-monthly, now only available online.

22. *Index of Conference Proceedings Received.* Boston Spa, British Library Document Supply Centre, 1964–. Monthly, with annual, five-, ten- and eighteen-year cumulations.

23. *Directory of Published Proceedings.* New York, Interdok Corp.
    Series MLS – Medical and Life Sciences, 1991–. Annual.
    Series PCE – Pollution Control and Ecology, 1974–. Semi-annual.
    Series SSH – Social Sciences / Humanities, 1968–. Quarterly.
    Series SEMT – Sciences, Engineering, Medicine and Technology, 1965–. Ten issues per year.

24. *Conference Papers Index.* Bethseda MD, Cambridge Scientific Abstracts, 1973–. Bi-monthly. (Cumulated in *Conference Papers Annual Index.*)

25. *Index to Scientific and Technical Proceedings.* Philadelphia, Institute for Scientific Information, 1978–. Monthly with annual cumulation.

26. *Index to Social Sciences and Humanities Proceedings.* Philadelphia, Institute for Scientific Information, 1979–. Quarterly with annual cumulation.

27. *Index to Theses Accepted for Higher Degrees by the Universities of Great Britain and Ireland.* London, ASLIB. Semi-annual.

28. *Dissertation Abstracts International.* Ann Arbor, University Microfilms Inc.
    Section A – Humanities and Social Sciences, 1938–. Monthly.

Section B – Sciences and Engineering, 1938–. Monthly.
Section C – Worldwide, 1976–. Quarterly.
Also available on CD-ROM and online.

29. *Chemical Abstracts*. Columbus, Ohio, American Chemical Society, 1907–. Weekly, with annual and five-year cumulative indexes. Also available online.

30. *Official Journal (Patents)*. Orpington, Patent Office. Weekly.

31. *Abstracts and Abridgements of Patent Specifications*. Orpington, Patent Office, 1883–. Weekly.

32. *World Patents Index*. London, Derwent, 1975–. Online.

33. *B.S.I. Standards Catalogue*. Milton Keynes, British Standards Institution, 1988. Annual, also on CD-ROM.

34. *I.S.O. Catalogue*. Geneva, International Organization for Standardization, 1999. Annual.

35. *PERINORM*. Bracknell, Technical Indexes Ltd. Annual with monthly updates.

36. AMERICAN NATIONAL STANDARDS INSTITUTE, *1998 Catalog of the American National Standards Institute*. Hitchen, American Technical Publishers, 1998. Annual.

37. *Annual Book of ASTM Standards*. Philadelphia, American Society for Testing and Materials (65 vols, each covering a different subject area).

38. BUTCHER, D.R., *Official Publications in Britain*. 2nd edn. London, Bingley, 1991.

39. *TSO Monthly Catalogue*. London, TSO.

40   *TSO Annual Catalogue*. London, TSO.

41. *UKOP, the Catalogue of United Kingdom Official Publications*. London, TSO & Chadwyck-Healey, 1989–. Quarterly.

42. http://www.the-stationery-office.co.uk

43. *Catalogue of British Official Publications not Published by TSO*. Cambridge, Chadwyck-Healey, 1980–. Bi-monthly.

44. CENTRAL STATISTICAL OFFICE, *Guide to Official Statistics*. London, TSO, 1996.

45. UNITED NATIONS DEPARTMENT OF INTERNA-
    TIONAL ECONOMIC & SOCIAL AFFAIRS, *Directory of
    International Statistics*. TSO, 1982. An irregular publication.

46. *ASLIB Directory of Information Sources in the United Kingdom*.
    10th edn. London, ASLIB, 1998.

47. *Directory of British Associations & Associations in Ireland*. 14th
    edn. Beckenham, CBD Research, 1998.

48. *Current Research in Britain*. 12th edn. London, Cartermill
    International, 1997 (4 vols – Physical sciences, Biological
    sciences, Social sciences and Humanities). Annual.

4

Electronic sources I – online searching

Online searching of bibliographic tools, or online information retrieval as it is commonly called, is a method of retrieving information from very large computer-mounted databases. Typically the computer is geographically remote from the intending user, who must use a terminal connected to the telephone and/or telecommunications networks to access the information. The modern online information retrieval industry is of central importance to anyone performing a literature search, whatever the subject may be. There are hundreds of bibliographic databases online covering every subject field. They provide access to millions of systematically organized references to all types of literature, journal and newspaper articles, reports, conferences, patents, standards, government publications, theses and dissertations. Many such databases are the direct online equivalent of printed bibliographies, others may represent a group of such bibliographies, while some have no printed equivalent and the information can only be accessed online. It is important to realize that the majority of this information is not available on the Internet except in the case of a host such as Dialog, which does provide access to its system via the Web. It is quite possible that more of the traditional online hosts will do this in order to access a wider market and take advantage of the popularity of Internet usage. This is perhaps necessary because, to the average researcher, the more traditional sources have become rather overshadowed by the cult of the Internet, which has benefited from immense publicity despite its limitations, and which has the advantage of easy public access.

In contrast, although most libraries, and certainly all academic libraries, will have online search facilities, the availability of these will vary a great deal. Sometimes the services are freely available to everybody, but it is more likely that they are offered only to staff or to staff and postgraduate students because of the high cost of this service. If undergraduates do have access to the service they may be asked to pay. The charges may be a nominal fixed fee of £10 to £20 or so, or the full cost may be required, which could be very substantial. Such charges may also apply to postgraduate students. It will be necessary to find out exactly what the position is in each library.

The idea of getting a substantial quality literature search carried out in a matter of minutes by a powerful computer is extremely tempting. Unfortunately, it is not as simple as this. There are enormous advantages in doing an online search, but equally there are very great disadvantages. It is as well to know something about the whole process in order to make a sensible decision as to whether this type of computer search will be helpful. It is also important to be able to assist the search process as much as possible. 'Garbage in – garbage out' is a principle which holds as much for online searching as for any other use of computers.

The development of online searching

The modern online information retrieval industry has evolved from relatively modest beginnings – the use of computers to assist in the compilation of indexes – and can be seen as part of an inexorable progression towards the computerization of all information. Rapid growth in the journal literature soon after the last war caused considerable problems to the producers of abstracting and indexing journals, as the provision of these services was at that time highly labour-intensive. There began to be unacceptable delays between the publication of a journal article and its inclusion in one of the bibliographic services. The production of annual and cumulative indexes to these sources showed even greater delays – up to two years or even more. It was the rapidly developing computer technology that came to the rescue. From the late 1950s and early 1960s, computers were increasingly used to compile the indexes of these services. At first they were used only to sort and manipulate the indexes, but very soon techniques of automatic indexing were developed that greatly speeded up the production of indexes. *Chemical Abstracts* and *Biological Abstracts* were two of the earliest pioneers in this field, and it is no coincidence that they are also two of the largest abstracting services in existence.

In order to allow the computer to do as much of the work as possible, it was necessary to put all the information into machine-readable form – bibliographic reference, abstract, indexing terms, and so on. It was therefore a logical development for the producers of these services to offer users the opportunity (at a cost) to request direct searches of the database. By repeating these searches every time new material was added to the database from update tapes it was also possible to offer a current awareness service. These early searches were done off-line in batch mode. That is, the users had to send in a description of the required search to a central point. A number of searches were run at one time, the information being fed into the computer by means of punched cards. There was no possibility of any interaction with the search process as it was being carried out, and the user was forced to wait for several days or even weeks before knowing whether the search had been successful or not. The service, therefore, although a great advance on anything that had been offered before, nevertheless had severe limitations.

Further evolution of computerized database systems was dependent on improvements in the computer and communications technology that took place in the 1970s and 1980s and which are still continuing. The most important developments that allowed the evolution of the modern information industry were:

● improvements in computer memory technologies that allow the construction of very large databases while still allowing very fast retrieval of the information;

- developments in hardware technology that enable simultaneous, interactive, online access to the databases by a very large number of users;

- developments in national and international telecommunications technology that enable users on the other side of the world to have access to these databases with a fast response time;

- improvements in the command languages to allow really sophisticated searching for experienced searchers and also a subsequent development of easier menu searching to attract untrained users.

The industry today continues to develop in parallel with advances in computer and telecommunications technology, and indeed the three sectors are mutually dependent to a considerable degree. However, there have been two significant developments over the last few years. First, there is a rapidly increasing trend for database producers and publishers to set up their own Web sites rather than lease their material to a supermarket online host. Second, in order to take advantage of the lure of the Internet, the traditional online hosts are now considering providing access to their systems via the Web. Because the full command language takes a while to learn, they are offering short-cut and menu systems that are easier for the novice to use, though there is a concomitant loss of sophistication in using such systems and results may well not be as good. However, it is not possible just to contact one of these Web sites and start searching. In order to search any of the hosts, a user must normally sign a contract or register on the Web page, undertaking to comply with the conditions laid down by the host as regards access, copyright, security and other issues, including fees if any. The traditional hosts will still require their users to have identification numbers and passwords. It is unusual, but not impossible, for an individual to contract with an online host, and a researcher with a reasonable budget and appropriate knowledge of searching might consider a personal membership. Organizational members are the norm, however, and there is usually a strict control over the online budget, otherwise the expense can quickly get out of hand.

The modern online industry

The structure of the online information industry may be considered as consisting of four independent but co-operating sections:

1. *The database producers* Those learned institutions, commercial companies or government bodies that traditionally have undertaken the task of producing bibliographic services in a particular subject field. These services are produced in printed and also in machine-readable form.

2. *The host* Also referred to as the *vendor* or *supplier*. This is a profit-making organization that purchases, or more usually leases, the machine-readable data from the producers. The databases are mounted individually on the host's own computer system. The host also provides the software necessary for searching the databases, and all the required technology for accessing the system via the national and international telecommunications networks.

   Some producers may act as their own vendors, though because of the fierce commercial pressures within this industry, this is often uneconomic. A host cannot normally survive by offering only one or two databases. In order to attract sufficient usage to support the high costs involved in offering online services, a reasonable number of databases must be on offer. It is because of this that there has been a recent trend for the big supermarket hosts to survive and for the smaller ones to disappear or to transfer to the Web or to CD-ROM.

3. *The telecommunications industry* This industry supplies cheap, reliable, long-distance, two-way communications channels through which users can contact the host from their own terminals. There are a number of such networks available that allow access to any host from almost any country in the world. Some online hosts, Dialog being one, are available via the Internet, but the speed of response does not compare at all well with the other networks available.

4. *The user* This has traditionally been a trained information professional searching on behalf of the person who actually requires the information (the 'end user'). This has been so because of the high costs of online searching. The theory is

that a specialist searcher will be able to perform searches more quickly and therefore more cheaply. However, in order to expand the potential number of users searching, hosts are now offering easier, user-friendly front end systems for the untrained searcher. They do profit from this as such users are normally much slower and try to browse, which means more time online and therefore more profit for the vendor.

The costs of online searching are certainly high. They involve payments to each section of the industry. In the first place, the host must be paid for the use of the database(s) accessed. This charge is based on the length of time the user is connected and varies according to the different databases. Some are relatively cheap, costing about £20 per hour, but some of the more expensive can cost up to £150 per hour and even more.

Second, the telecommunications charges must be paid, and these are calculated partly on the length of time of the connection and partly on the number of characters passing to and fro on the channel. Finally, the telephone charge for the connection to the local telecommunications mode must be added. The expense of an online search can therefore be considerable when all these costs are taken into account. A very rough estimate of average cost would be £1 per minute online.

Because of the expense involved, academic libraries are highly unlikely to allow researchers to do their own searches. In order to keep costs down the person doing the search should be properly trained and able to perform fast but effective searches. A member of the library staff will therefore act as an intermediary, who will also be able to use the full command language that will enable a far more sophisticated search to be done than can be achieved with the simplified menu systems. The client will need to give the details of the required search to the librarian who will then prepare and carry it out. From the client's point of view this may not be entirely satisfactory, but before discussing this further it is as well to review the advantages and disadvantages of online searching generally.

Advantages

1. *Speed of retrieval*   This is probably the overriding attraction for any researcher. Twenty or 30 years of an abstracting journal can be searched in a few minutes online. Even allowing for the necessary off-line preparation, an extensive search will take a fraction of the time needed for a manual search. Searching through a direct telecommunications channel such as Tymnet or Telenet is very much faster than through the Internet, which is becoming very slow and at peak times can come to a standstill.

2. *Quality*   Nearly all the material on offer has come from the traditional publishing system which means that the producers are reputable and, in the case of journal literature, much of the material will have been refereed by subject experts or at least by editors in the initial stages of acceptance. The reliability and accuracy of the material is therefore high.

3. *Range*   Online services offer access to a wide range of databases, many more than the average library can subscribe to in hard (printed) copy format. This means that researchers can broaden their search far beyond the limits of the library. There are also increasing numbers of databases that are not available in any other format.

4. *Access to the references*   Whereas in the majority of printed sources a reference will be indexed under the author's name and only two or three subject terms, the number of access points to a computer record is far greater. In theory, any word in any field of the record may be used as a search term. In practice, each database differs in respect of the searchable fields and must be checked before the search is prepared to see what is offered. It should be possible to search for any word in the title, abstract (if present) and descriptor fields, but also it may be possible to search by such fields as language, country of publication, journal title, date, and so forth. In a printed source, the actual reference must be scanned to select by these criteria.

5. *Printouts*   It is possible to print out an online search as it is being performed, and also to order a printed copy of the references resulting from the search. This copy will be produced

by the host and mailed to the user. It will normally arrive within a week. This facility can reduce or even eliminate the note-taking that is unavoidable in a manual search.

6. *Interactive searching*   This means that a search can be altered in response to the results obtained. In order to have such an input into the search the researcher would, of course, have to be present as it is being carried out and this is not always possible. It is worth asking the person who is carrying out the search to allow the user to be there also. Some intermediaries actively encourage such participation, as they can get an instant response from the user regarding the relevance of the results being obtained. This is as useful to them as it is to the user.

7. *Current awareness services*   Most online hosts offer not only retrospective search facilities but also current awareness or update facilities. When a satisfactory search strategy has been worked out it can be stored in the computer permanently. The host will then automatically run the search against every update made to the database(s) specified and if any new references are retrieved a printout will be sent to the user.

8. *Downloading*   Depending on the technology – both hardware and software – that is available to the searcher, it should be possible to download the details of the references retrieved to a printer, to floppy disc, or directly to the computer's word-processing facility where it may be edited as required. It will be necessary to check the copyright stipulations of both the host and the database to ensure that such downloading is legal. It should also be remembered that much downloading in this way will increase the costs of the search substantially as both the connect time and the number of bits transferred over the network contribute to the total costs. It is therefore cheaper to use the online print facilities, which means that the search results will be printed out locally and mailed to the searcher. This only takes a very few days.

9. *Document delivery*   This service is offered by most online hosts, or by the individual databases. It means that printed journal articles and other items identified during the search can also be ordered online. The documents will be mailed to the user. Unfortunately the service tends to be expensive, much more so than the traditional British Library document

supply system. In the UK, therefore, academic and public libraries are not particularly keen to use this facility.

Disadvantages

1. *Poor and inconsistent indexing*   When applied to the database records this can cause severe problems by making it harder to perform a comprehensive search. Any deficiency in indexing becomes far more noticeable online than it does in a printed tool. This is partly because it is possible to skim through a printed index picking out all the likely headings, and taking account of any 'see' and 'see also' references. To browse in an equivalent fashion online is a much less reliable process and so it is more difficult to counter inconsistencies. The indexing is usually the responsibility of the original producer, not the host, although some hosts do enhance the indexing of some of their databases. In addition, any scan of the dictionary indexes will reveal numerous typographical errors, and the misspelling of a keyword can mean that the item will not be retrieved by the literal-minded computer. Fortunately, really poor indexing is not often found.

2. *Retrospective searching*   This is frequently restricted compared to a printed source, which will often go back much further than the online version. To search back 20 or 30 years is probably ample for many subjects, especially in the sciences, medicine and technologies. However, such a limit may be a severe restriction in the humanities and social sciences.

3. *Bias*   This occurs in two ways. The arts and humanities, and to a lesser extent the social sciences, are far less well represented in terms of number of databases online than are the sciences and technologies, which have excellent coverage. Business databases have rapidly increased over the last few years and this subject is also well served. Bias also appears in the origins of much of the online information, there being a distinct US domination. The British and European online industry lagged behind that of the United States for some years, but is now catching up rapidly, and this bias is not as

great as it once was. However, it will always exist to an extent merely because of the difference in quantity of material published in the two areas. However, if a searcher requires references relating only to the United Kingdom there can sometimes be difficulty in separating these out online, as many databases, like their printed equivalents, are international in scope.

4. *Need for an intermediary*   As explained above, in order to perform a sophisticated online search quickly, with a high rate of retrieval of relevant references, it is necessary to have some training and expertise in the full command language. For this reason, most researchers will have to make use of an intermediary. One of the problems resulting from this is that the intermediary is almost certainly not going to be as fully conversant as the user with what is required. A briefing will certainly be requested and the ultimate success of the search will depend largely on the quality of information exchanged at this session. If the intermediary is not very skilled at such a task, and if the user has no understanding of the online process, then the results of the search can be very disappointing.

It may also happen that the intermediary is not a very efficient online searcher. Most people can grasp the logic of online searching and learn the basic commands, but this is not enough. Good searching depends very much on the intermediary having a wide vocabulary, an appreciation of language and semantics, and a flexibility of mind that can manipulate the system being used – a sort of online lateral thinking. Unfortunately, many searchers do not have these skills and, although they can perform a very literal search that will retrieve a number of useful references, they may miss more than they find. The number of references that have *not* been discovered will, of course, never be known. It is impossible to judge the quality of an online search on the results of that search alone.

5. *The advent of menu systems*   This has enabled users to do their own searching but it is not possible to do such a sophisticated search in this mode. It is also necessary to realize that not all databases may be accessed with this method of searching, especially when databases have been organized into groups that are searched as if they comprise a single source. Often

these groups comprise only the larger and more general sources and other smaller or more specialist sources cannot be accessed in this way.

How online searches work

If, after due consideration of the pros and cons of the traditional online searching, it is decided to make use of this facility, then, as in the case of the Internet, it is helpful to have some idea of what the computer does. The online search does not work in quite the same way as a manual search, basically because it has no intelligence to apply to the task as has a human. Just as it is necessary to have an understanding of the bibliographic organization in order to search the printed literature effectively, so it is necessary during a computer search to know something about the organization and manipulation of the records on the database.

A bibliographic database consists of a very large number of references that in many cases are accompanied by an abstract. The complete entry for any one document consists of a number of standard elements of information – author, title, journal, abstract, index terms, and so on. In computer jargon the whole entry is known as a record and each component element of information is a field. The complete collection of records is known as a file. Often the term file is used interchangeably with database, but in reality each database consists of a number of files. A printed database such as an abstracting journal allows its records to be accessed through a relatively small number of index terms. However, in machine-readable form the record is amenable to manipulation in many different ways and will allow access through almost any field or part of a field. In order to see how this is done it is necessary to examine briefly the database structure. Basically, this structure is built up from three types of file, the *bibliographic* file and two supporting files, the *dictionary* and *inverted* files.

The bibliographic file

This is the main file of bibliographic records organized in numerical order using the accession number. Typically, this indicates a year and abstract number which correspond to the year and abstract number used for that particular record in the printed equivalent, if there is one. This useful feature allows easy cross-referencing between the online and printed database.

It will be obvious that a file of several hundred thousand records arranged in numerical order is not very easy to search by author or subject, or indeed any element apart from the accession number. To do so would require the computer to search every single record in order to locate those that matched the parameters given to it. This would be time-consuming, extremely expensive and a generally inefficient use of the computer's time. To get over this problem, the bibliographic file is never searched directly. In fact the database can only be searched by means of the supporting or *auxiliary* files that act as indexes to the main file.

The dictionary file

This file consists of an alphabetical sequence of all the directly searchable terms in the main file. Against each is given the number of records (postings) which contain that term (see Table 4.1).

The dictionary file is the first to be accessed when the computer

Table 4.1   Section of dictionary file

Bank	42
Banking	63
Bank loan	84
Bank loans	462
Banks	102
Business	72
Computer	37
Computer-based	14
Computerized	21
Computers	168
.	
.	
.	
.	
.	
Students	253

is asked to search for a term, for example 'bank loans'. It inspects the list and if it finds a match it will print out the number of postings. In this case there are 462 records containing the required term. Suppose a search was being made for articles about bank loans to students. At this stage of the search, there is no indication of how many of those 462 references will be relevant. The computer can be asked to search for the term 'students' and it will come back with another set of postings, say 253. However, what the searcher really wants to know is how many references are indexed by the term 'bank loans' and the term 'students'. In order to discover this, the computer must access the other auxiliary file.

The inverted file

The inverted file tells the computer which individual bibliographic records make up the postings for a particular term shown in the dictionary file. It consists of an alphabetical list of search terms exactly as before, but here, instead of the number of postings, are listed all the accession numbers of the records (see Table 4.2). Thus, if the dictionary file shows 63 postings, there will be 63 individual accession numbers against that term in the inverted file.

It is now possible to work out how the computer can manipulate a search to locate individual references. If a single term is asked for, the computer will first display the number of postings and then, if it is asked to display some or all of those postings, it will access the inverted file, read off the required accession numbers and search the bibliographic file for those numbers. When it has found the records it will then display them. Although this

Table 4.2   Section of inverted file

Bank	85567823, 85214398, 84239856, 83753957, 83127635, ...
Banking	85263745, 85002341, 83456172, 83027346, 82354612, ...
Bank loan	85354672, 84352617, 84245361, 83201980, 81348912, ...
Bank loans	85263745, 85134523, 85027346, 84275678, 83567098, ...
.	
.	
.	
Students	86445679, 85354672, 85263745, 84765879, 84275678, ...

requires three searches on the part of the computer, each search is a very easy and fast operation and is more efficient than attempting to search the bibliographic records directly.

Combining search terms

It is relatively rare that a search can be completed satisfactorily by using only single search terms. Usually the topic that is being searched for can only be expressed using a number of search terms. In order to combine these in the appropriate way, the searcher uses what are known as *Boolean operators* or *logical operators*. These operators are merely instructions using the words 'OR', 'AND' and 'NOT'. Boolean operators are also used on CD-ROMs and by Internet search engines, so it is important to understand how they work.

The OR operator is used to build a set that represents a single concept by using the various synonyms and related terms that can be used to express that concept. It causes the computer to select references containing any or all of the terms that are being ORed together. This is necessary because the computer is completely literal. If it is asked to look for the term 'bank' it will do so, but will not look for the term 'banks' unless it is specifically asked to do so. The following Venn diagram (Figure 4.1) illustrates the use of the OR operator being used to build a set containing the term 'bank loan' and 'bank loans'.

The shaded area in Sets 1 and 2 represents the references that contain the term being searched for. There will be some references that contain both words in the record and this is shown by the double-hatched area in Set 3. The final number of references that would be retrieved is shown by the whole shaded area in Set 3.

When asked to implement an OR operator, the computer accesses the inverted file for all the terms that are being ORed together and will combine the various lists of accession numbers into one set, which it will then store separately. Accession numbers that appear under more than one term will only be counted once, so duplicates are eliminated. The effect of the OR operator is thus to increase the number of items retrieved, and is used to

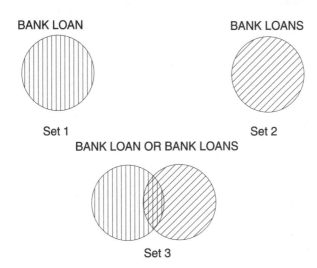

Figure 4.1   Use of the OR operator

retrieve all items concerning a particular concept that may have been indexed under a variety of terms.

There is no limit to the number of search terms that can be ORed together, but they *must* represent the same concept at the same level of specificity otherwise disaster may result. Thus, 'child abuse', 'battered babies' and 'battered children' may be ORed together, but the single words 'abuse' or 'battered' should not be included. This would retrieve references concerned with drug abuse, alcohol abuse, battered wives, and so on, which is getting away from the desired topic. In fact many, if not most, concepts are better expressed by phrases of two, three or even more words, and the search languages all offer the facility for precise searching for these word strings.

The AND operator, in the second Venn diagram (Figure 4.2), selects from two or more existing sets those references which contain all of the terms that are being ANDed together. It will eliminate those records which contain only one of the terms required.

The shaded area in Set 5 indicates the references that match with the topic 'bank loans to students'. Each reference will contain at least one of the terms relating to bank loans *and* at least one term that relates to students. The AND operator is therefore used to

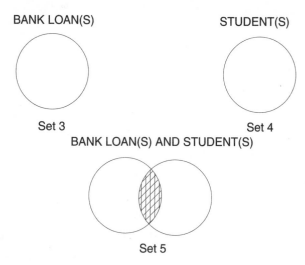

Figure 4.2   Use of the AND operator

create a set that represents a combination of concepts. It causes the number of references to decrease, and the subject specificity of those references to increase.

The implementation of the AND operator by the computer requires it to access the lists of accession numbers under each of the terms being ANDed together and to match the lists together. Whenever it finds the same number in each list, that number is copied into a new set. For example, for a search on bank loan(s) to students in the index illustrated in Table 4.2, the references with the accession numbers 85354672, 85263745 and 84275678 would be identified in this way.

The NOT operator is implemented in a similar way, except that in this case the computer will eliminate those references that contain the NOTed term(s).

This description of how an online search works has been considerably simplified, but is useful in that it helps to illustrate the basic difference between manual and computer searching. With manual searching the indexes nearly always give an indication of the context in which the index term is being used. They do this by using sub-headings, the title, added index terms and also provide *see* and *see also* references to help the searcher. On the other hand, the computer search is relying not on context but on proximity of the search terms in the references. This reliance on proximity can cause quite unintentional and hilarious mistakes. For example, a search on the ecology of woods and woodland retrieved an enormous number of articles on marine biology. Why? Because the authors of these papers worked at the Woods Hole Marine Biological Laboratory. The computer dutifully picked up the words 'woods' and 'ecology' in each paper, and that was that as far as it was concerned. It is necessary to design a search strategy with some care to avoid these 'false drops'. It is impossible to exclude them entirely, but a good searcher can produce a much more precise set of results than a careless one.

In addition to the basic principles of searching, there are all sorts of additional commands that enable the searcher to specify such things as phrases, where in the record (for example the title) the search terms are to be, what dates, languages, publications, countries, type of document are required. It is also possible to search more than one database at a time, to eliminate duplicate records when doing so, to sort and rank information, and so on. The command languages are constantly being improved and updated in order to allow more and more sophisticated manipulation of the search and of the information retrieved.

It must therefore be appreciated that the preparation and execution of an online search should be done with great care and the person who requires the search can help the intermediaries very much by giving them precise and full information about the topic. Usually, the user and the intermediary will meet to discuss the search, but some libraries still ask for a search request form to be filled in and work from this rather than from an interview.

Whichever method is used, the user should be prepared with the following information:

1. A clear definition of the topic to be searched. This should be encapsulated in one sentence – not always an easy task, but it does help to clarify the mind.
2. Identification of the different concepts and their relationship within the topic. It helps to rank the concepts in order of their importance, as it may not be possible to use all of them in the search.
3. The background of the search and the reason why the search

has been requested. It may be that an online search is inappropriate and, if so, an alternative strategy could be suggested.

4. A list of search terms for each concept including related terms and synonyms. If the AND and OR operators are understood this list is likely to be more comprehensive.

5. If a key reference(s) is known, give the details. It may be possible to retrieve this online and see how it has been indexed.

6. An indication of how exhaustive the search should be and how many references can be coped with. It is not unusual for a search to produce several hundred or even several thousand references. If these cannot be dealt with then it makes sense to reduce the number by making the search more specific in some way.

7. Which languages are acceptable.

8. What time period should be covered.

9. What types of document are required. It may be possible to restrict the search to journals, patents, conferences, etc. or alternatively to exclude one or more of these formats.

10. Any other restrictions. For example, terms definitely not wanted in the search but which might occur in conjunction with desired terms.

11. Date by which results are required.

12. Which manual sources have already been searched.

If a search profile has already been constructed as suggested in Chapter 2 then all of these points should have already been considered, and if some manual searching has been done then the information that can be given to the intermediary will be as complete as can be. This will lead to the best possible results being obtained from the online search.

Searching on CD-ROM

It is important to know how classic online searching works even though it is not so likely that researchers will be able to do it for themselves. A format that will, however, be constantly used is the CD-ROM as this is now so commonly found. The user interface to be found on the majority of CD-ROMs has been made as simple as possible by the publishers. Therefore, although Boolean operators are being used, this is not always completely obvious, in that rather than the users being expected to type in ANDs and ORs, they may possibly be given prompts such as 'add another keyword'. In the search for simplicity, there has had to be a sacrifice in terms of sophistication of the strategies that can be used on a CD-ROM and it is better to keep a search as simple as possible. Most of the comments made above about searching online are equally valid for CD-ROM but, as the search software can differ quite a lot between publishers, it is a good idea to read the instructions offered, although admittedly these can be somewhat sparse and unhelpful.

There has been little published about CD-ROM search technique but there is one very useful book by Meloche (1) that is useful to both the novice and the more experienced CD-ROM searcher. This not only covers the general principles of searching but examines the products and search techniques for a number of major American publishers of abstracts and indexing journals on CD-ROM.

Reference

1.   MELOCHE, J., *Introductory CD ROM searching; the key to effective ondisc searching*. New York, Haworth Press, 1994.

5

Electronic sources II – the Internet

These days it would appear that nobody is anybody unless they use the Internet as an information source, and indeed it is certainly a valuable tool to have at one's disposal. However, as with classic online searching, it is important to have a critical understanding of how to best exploit its facilities. There is a common misconception, especially among younger people, that all information, or at any rate all the information that matters, is to be found on the Internet. Other misconceptions are that the use of the Internet costs nothing, that the Internet and the Web are one and the same, that search engines all search the whole of the Internet in the same way and that there is no need to use any other sources of information. No doubt these misunderstandings have arisen for a number of reasons. There is undeniably a huge amount of information on this source, but it is also true that there has been almost a cult built up around it and there is strong social and political pressure to have access to it. Government, schools, colleges and universities, sales and marketing personnel, software producers, the service providers and telecommunications industries and many other sections of society who have a financial or propagandist interest in the Internet have all been heavily promoting its use. Much of this promotion has been through self-interest and it is only fairly recently that a more critical look has been taken at the information available and the access to it, and such studies often do not show such enthusiasm.

One of the most important points to realize is that the Internet is *by no means* the complete substitute for all the more traditional print and electronic sources of information. The greatest mistake that a researcher can make is to assume that the Internet is a one-stop shop of information, substituting for and/or incorporating everything that has ever been published in whatever form. This is far from true and any serious literature search should concentrate on the traditional sources or much important work will be missed. Rather, the Internet should be regarded as a new source, offering new sorts of information, which extends and complements the more traditional sources. There is, of course, a degree of overlap that is increasing all the while as print and classic electronic sources are made available through the Internet, but this overlap is tiny when considered in relation to the sheer size and volume of information offered.

Anyone who has attempted to search for specific information on the Internet will be well aware that, unless the specific address (uniform resource locator or URL) of a site is already known, it can be both difficult and time-consuming to locate appropriate information. There are a large number of books available to both the novice and more experienced Internet user such as the well-known *Internet for Dummies* (1). Particularly useful for anyone wishing to search seriously are Barrett's *NetResearch* (2) and Fielden's *Internet Research* (3), which both cover techniques of Internet searching and give useful pointers towards sites of electronic libraries. There are also two titles primarily aimed at information professionals, therefore offering a great many tips on searching as well as lists of sites, services, links and gateways that will lead to the most informative parts of the Internet from an academic point of view. These are *The Library and Information Professional's Guide to the Internet* (4), which is British, and *Internet Connections* (5), which is an American publication and has a useful list of electronic journals, though this, like all such lists, will inevitably date quickly. However, the technology of searching is outside the scope of this book and this chapter will concentrate instead on a slightly more analytical and evaluative consideration of Internet searching.

As is the case with all sources, browsing the Internet can be fun, and quite often information is found serendipitously, but this activity is just as likely to be totally unproductive and waste a lot of time and the serious searcher can end up very frustrated. Part of this frustration can be relieved if the searcher understands a little of what is going on when a search engine is asked to perform a search and so has more realistic expectations of what can be achieved and can apply better techniques. Most activity on the Internet concerns the World Wide Web and so that will be the major consideration here, although there are other sources which will be considered later. Web searching is done using one or more of the search engines provided. There are dozens of these, all of which differ from one another.

What is a search engine?

A search engine is a software program which has been designed to locate and retrieve Web documents in response to a user's request. A search engine is necessary because the Web has no other form of indexing. It is an unstructured source where sites are constantly appearing, disappearing and changing address. Search engines have been designed to try to cope with this transitory nature. There are several different types which may be broadly classified by the way in which they search and also by what they search for. It is clearly an advantage to searchers to know what type of search engine they are currently using as this will affect both the search strategy and the results.

Automated search engines

Also known as statistical search engines, these are the oldest and include most of the largest (in the sense of number of sites indexed) search engines, including Altavista, Hotbot, Lycos and Web Crawler. They are comprised of the following components:

1. *The robot* finds and retrieves new resources. Robots are continually searching for new documents (sites), but the robot belonging to one search engine will not find exactly the same

sites as another, nor the same number. Thus by using different search engines, a searcher will be accessing a different group of documents.

2.   *The indexer* is a software program that will automatically extract keywords from each document that are added to the index. It is these words that will be matched with a user's query. The indexer indexes every significant word of the document (full text indexing) and assigns relative weightings to each meaningful word by means of an algorithm. The weightings assigned will depend not only on the frequency of occurrence in the document but also upon the number of times that word already occurs in the index.

The basic assumption is, of course, that the more times a word occurs in the text, the more likely it is to reflect the topic that the document is about. This is, however, a tremendous generalization and it is quite possible for a word to appear many times yet not be particularly relevant to the main topic. The word 'computer', for example, will crop up in many articles that are not about computers as such. The indexer will therefore also look not only at the number of times a word appears in the document but also at the average number of occurrences in the index. If this is high in comparison to the document then the word is not going to be so useful in distinguishing that document from others and will be given a lower weighting. However, if the occurrence in the index is far lower than in the document then it will be a more significant word for identifying that document and will get a higher weighting.

3.   *The index* is where all the weighted keywords are stored with pointers towards the corresponding documents.

4.   *The searcher* will take users' search queries and match up the terms used with those in the index, and the results will be presented to the searcher with the highest weighted documents coming at the top of the list.

5.   *Metadata* is the term used for the information that describes each resource and corresponds roughly to the entry in a library catalogue. It will include such elements as title, author, copyright holder, description, key index terms, URL, date when last modified, and so on.

A statistical search engine tries to identify vocabulary that discriminates between documents but it is clear that this method is hardly an exercise in precision indexing. Because common terms will get low weightings, their use will tend to cause huge numbers of not very relevant documents to be retrieved. It is also the reason why the most relevant documents to the user often occur quite low down in the rankings and may be missed, especially if the total recall runs to several hundred or even several thousand items. Few people have the patience to scan down so far in the list. Because of this disadvantage, other types of search engine have been developed.

Classified directories

This type of search engine has been developed in an effort to overcome some of the disadvantages of the automated version. As automatically generated metadata, and particularly the indexing, can be inaccurate or at any rate unhelpful, the classified directories use manually defined metadata and manual classification. Yahoo and EINet Galaxy are two such systems and they work on similar principles to the classifications schemes to be found in libraries. Index terms are matched up with a classification scheme and the document allocated a classification number. As this is done by humans the precision is likely to be high. The searcher will then likewise match up the user's terms with the scheme and will access all the documents that are clustered at the appropriate location. This method will always be more accurate than a purely automated system and the retrieved items should be more relevant. Furthermore, users are able to browse the classification scheme themselves and use their existing knowledge and intuition to further the search.

Subject specific gateways

This development allows a search within a predefined group of subject-related sites, which is helpful because there is less need to consider that the terminology used could be found with somewhat different meanings in material relating to a different topic. SOSIG (Social Science Information Gateway) is an example. A number of general search engines also offer a similar facility, such as EINet Galaxy and Virtual Library.

Geographically restricted engines

There are a number of search engines that index only those documents that relate to a particular geographic area such as Europe or the UK. In the case of many searches it is preferred that only British material, for example, is required and this can be difficult to extract from a general facility as US material dominates on the Internet. Search engines such as Euroferret or UK Index should be tried in such cases. Some of the big names, for example Yahoo, also offer a facility to restrict a search to the UK but these frequently do not seem to be effective.

Automated classified directory

The advantage of automated search engines is precisely that they are automatic and can work more quickly and cheaply than humans. Research is currently in progress to try to combine the advantages of automated with those of classified directories. It is based on the Dewey Decimal System as that is familiar to so many people and hopefully will show a substantial advance on current systems in terms of accuracy.

Meta search engines

These do not search directly for sites themselves. They operate by passing the query on to a group of search engines which may number anything from half a dozen or so to twenty or more. By using meta search engines the user will retrieve much more, indeed far more than most people can deal with, but, equally, the number of irrelevant documents will also be very great and there are often many duplicates as well. In addition, it seems to be very difficult to refine the search adequately.

Meta tags

Not a search engine at all, but another approach to solving the problem of automatically generated metadata. The use of meta tags means that the authors specify their own metadata which allows for greater accuracy and the inclusion of search terms that may not necessarily appear in the document. A good idea, but an unfortunate development has been that authors keen to advertise their sites as widely as possible incorporate all sorts of unlikely terms, and also links, so that users can be led into their sites even when the topic is not really relevant.

Tips for Internet searching

From the discussion above, it becomes clear that the precision of searching available on the Internet does not match that of classic online searching as discussed in the preceding chapter, and that somewhat different strategies may have to be applied to obtain reasonable results. It may be useful to summarize some suggestions for Internet searching.

1. Find out what category the search engines you are using fall into. This is not always possible from the home page and it may be necessary to have recourse to a source that describes and reviews search engines. There are a number of these in books, journals and on the Web itself.
2. Use a variety of search engines. Different results will be obtained from each on the same search and it may well be that certain ones tend to be more consistently successful for particular topics.
3. It is better to use rare or unusual search terms as these produce better results than common ones. Their occurrence in the documents may be low but concomitantly their weighting will be high and the retrieved information is likely to be more relevant. It is also helpful to use a group of synonyms as authors invariably try to use them rather than repeat the same word or phrase to the point of irritation.
4. For similar reasons, it is a good idea to search for phrases wherever possible because these are not only more specific in their meaning but carry a meaning that is different from that of their constituent words. For example, the phrases 'paper tiger', 'organic farming' and 'red herring' all have very

different meanings from either of their two words considered individually. The Boolean AND would not be helpful in such cases.

5. Always look for and use the so-called advanced search facilities. These are actually very basic compared with online searching but cover the same elementary functions such as Boolean operators and proximity operators. These facilities are often not immediately apparent on the home page and it is usually necessary to look for them under a heading such as 'search tips', or 'advanced search'.

6. Do try and search at a time when the Internet is not being really heavily used. For us in the UK this will normally be at a time when the US is asleep – in other words in the morning – when the response time will be reasonable. Otherwise it can be frustratingly slow.

Other facilities on the Internet

Although most heavily used, the Web is not the only facility on the Internet. Rather it is the most recent and glamorous, and it is perhaps worth briefly mentioning the existence of some other facilities that may be as, or possibly even more, useful for a literature searcher, depending on the sort of information required. In particular, Barrett's book (2) offers some addresses at which information about and lists of sites may be found for each of the following, which are certainly worth exploring:

1. *FTP* or File Transfer Protocol is an old method used for sending files from one computer to another and FTP sites are mostly used for downloading freeware and shareware. Most have the point and click graphical interfaces familiar to Web users and can be accessed via the Web. The searcher can also download FTP files which are presented as links, and it is just a matter of clicking on the required link.

2. *Gopher sites* are considerably more limited than the Web in that they are text only sources and can link only to other gopher pages. Most Web browsing programs can also access Gopher, but it is a system which is slowly becoming obsolete. Despite that, there is still some interesting information there.

3. *Usenet* is the network that allows worldwide discussion groups known as newsgroups that each concentrate on a specific topic. It is possible just to read the articles posted or to post one's own article, which could be a request for information.

Manual versus online versus Internet searching

There has been a long-standing debate about the effectiveness of online searching as compared to manual searching, and a number of detailed comparisons have been made. It seems to have been widely established that if the same search is performed in both modes then the results are not the same. In fact, one early study by Hartley (6) found that the degree of overlap was only 21 per cent for all references and as little as 12 per cent for the really relevant references. In other words, only a tiny minority of the useful references were retrieved by both the manual and the online search. More disturbingly, a later research study (7) has found that online searching gives the poorer result when compared with manual methods. In this instance, online searches were only able to identify just over 25 per cent of the references retrieved manually from bibliographies, and roughly 50 per cent of those retrieved from individual abstracting and indexing journals. The main reason for this is that the computer brings no intelligence to the search as a manual searcher does. A human has the understanding of context and of the subject itself that allows recognition of unusual language that nevertheless refers to the correct topic. However, it requires experience to translate this understanding into an effective search strategy.

Some research (see also Table 5.1) has now been carried out comparing online and Internet searching (8). Briefly, this has shown that searching takes far longer on the Web (more than double the time) and, although the total amount of information retrieved was greater, the material retrieved online had a greater relevance, at least when scanning the top layer of results. In fact the Internet did produce relevant material but this was often ranked well down in the hierarchy of results and under normal search circumstances is liable to be overlooked. Most searchers

Table 5.1   A comparison of some of the advantages and disadvantages of online and Internet searching

Online	Internet
1 The range of sources is more restricted, but for academic topics it is almost certain that some information will be found. A zero result is most likely to be due to either a faulty search strategy or an incorrect choice of database.	1 There is a huge variety of sources but only overlapping with online to a relatively small extent, and much of the traditional academic information is not on the Internet. Finding desired information can be a much more chancy business. The Internet is not just an information resource, though, as it also provides a number of major forms of communication.
2 Quality of information may be relied upon as it has been through the traditional selection/refereeing and checking process.	2 On the majority of sites there is no control on quality, accuracy or reliability of the information. Some sites are dependable, others are inaccurate, dated, deliberately misleading or downright crazy. Most of this information has not gone through any quality checking procedure. There are reliable documents, for example refereed electronic journals or sites of well-known organizations, but it behoves the user to be very discriminating.
3 The indexing is detailed, accurate and consistent and repeat searches will bring up the identical information.	3 Indexing systems are highly variable. Not only will different results be obtained from the same strategy used on different search engines, but even the same search repeated on the same database is likely to produce different results.
4 The command languages, once learnt, allow the most precise and sophisticated searching offered by any electronic source and the searcher can adjust the degree of sophistication or of specificity	4 The search process is in one sense easier but it is also far less sophisticated and it is not possible to obtain the same degree of relevance. It is also difficult on many search engines to adjust the search strategy *continued*

Table 5.1 *Concluded*

Online	Internet
immediately in response to the number and relevance of the items retrieved.	cumulatively and it may be necessary to start from scratch with a new search.
5 There are consistent record formats within a database and across similar databases on the same host, and even across hosts the differences are very slight. This makes locating specific information within the record very easy.	5 There is no consistency at all between sites or even between different parts of the same site in most cases. This makes scanning and picking out the required information a more time-consuming process.
6 Currency is variable between databases but the frequency and date of last update is shown in the headers and on the database sheets.	6 Currency is very variable as it depends much more on the inclination of the creator of the site. Not all sites show date of last update.
7 Speed of searching at off-peak times is very good, especially on a direct telecommunications channel.	7 Speed of searching can be dire at peak times and even at less busy times can still be poor for popular sites. This is an increasing problem because of the continuing huge growth of traffic on the system.
8 Online searching is expensive. Although there are often discounts available for heavy users, the more it is used the bigger the bill.	8 Internet access is provided for an annual subscription to the service provider and does not thereafter depend on the amount of use. However, not all the information on the Internet is free.
9 Online files are normally text only. It is rare to find any sort of graphics.	9 The use of colour, graphics and even sound is common and thus information can be offered in certain formats only found elsewhere on CD-ROMs.

have neither the time nor the inclination to scan several hundred references to pick out the gold from the dross. Possibly the most important finding, however, is that there was very little duplication among the items retrieved.

The lesson to be learned from such results is that if a thorough literature search is required (as distinct from some representative references) then multiple formats should be used. Print, online and Internet are offering different types of literature and should be regarded as complementary. The combination of formats chosen for any particular literature search will depend on various factors, including time factors, costs, availability, range and quantity of material required, level of expertise available, and so on. Probably the best compromise would be to do a manual or CD-ROM search of those tools that are available to hand, an online search for those that would otherwise be inaccessible and a top-up scan of the Internet as a more speculative venture.

References

1.   LEVINE, J.L., *The Internet for Dummies*. 5th edn. Foster City CA, IDG Books, 1998.

2.   BARRETT, D.J., *NetResearch; finding information online*. Sebastopol GA, O'Reilly, 1997.

3.   FIELDEN, N.L. and GARRIDO, M., *Internet Research; theory and practice*. Jefferson NC, McFarland, 1998.

4.   TSENG, G. et al., *The Library and Information Professional's Guide to the Internet*. London, Library Association, 1996.

5.   ENGLE, M.E., *Internet Connections; a librarian's guide to dial-up access and use*. Chicago, LITA, 1995.

6.   HARTLEY, D., A laboratory method for the comparison of retrieval effectiveness in manual and online searching. IN *Proceedings of the 7th International Online Information Meeting*. Oxford, Learned Information, 1983.

7.   DAVISON, P.S. et al., *International Bibliographic Review on Costs and Modelling in Information Retrieval*. London, British Library, 1988. (British Library Research Paper 37.)

8.   FELDMAN, S., The Internet Search-Off. *Searcher* 6(2), Feb. 1998, pp. 28–35.

6

Keeping records

The need to keep clear and accurate records during a literature search cannot be overemphasized. Many people seem to consider that keeping a written record of progress is a tedious and time-consuming activity that has little value. Often these people think that they can safely rely on memory or an occasional note. However, every reference librarian has learned to dread the production by a distraught client of scrappy pieces of paper covered with impromptu shorthand scribbles that have subsequently defied both translation and memory. By the time it is realized that proper records are essential, the search may have got into such a tangle that much of the work has to be redone, and a good deal of time has been wasted. The effort required to keep really useful records is not, in fact, very great, and the investment of the time necessary for this activity will be repaid many times over.

Quite apart from the personal advantage accrued, good records will allow students in particular to show their supervisor exactly what they have accomplished and how they are progressing. The supervisor is then likely to be able to give more pertinent advice than if he or she has only the haziest notion of what has been done. Similarly, if librarians are approached for assistance at any time, their job will also be made much easier if they can see the progress record to date.

There are many ways in which records can be kept, and the method chosen should match the way an individual thinks and works as far as possible. It should also suit the sorts of information that need to be recorded. This may vary somewhat depending on the subject and scope of a literature search, and any method chosen may require a certain amount of adaptation. However, whatever system is chosen, it should be able to record such information as the sources that have been searched, references that have been found and documents, including photocopies, that have been collected, in a way that is both simple and flexible.

Recording the search

It frequently does not occur to researchers to keep a record of what has been done in the course of a literature search, as distinct from what references have been found. However, if such a record is not kept, it is all too easy to waste time and effort by searching sources that have already been examined. Conversely, it may happen that a potential source or part of a source is inadvertently omitted from the search because it is not on the library shelf for some reason when the main search takes place. In addition, the need to check incoming issues of sources such as indexing and abstracting journals is often overlooked in the latter phases of research. It is necessary to monitor the literature throughout, and to remember that it seems to be a law of literature searches that the source not looked at, for whatever reason, is the one that contains an essential reference. A simple search record will take only a very few minutes to maintain and will act as a useful memory jogger, ensuring that none of the above problems occur.

The information that should be recorded about the search includes:

1. *The title and location of the source to be searched*   This note should include any changes of title; for example, *Current Technology Index* used to be called *British Technology Index*. It may be that the different titles are shelved in different places and this is often overlooked.

2. *The year from which the search is to start in that source* It is possible that the run of the required source does not go back to this date in one particular library. Alternatively, it is now a common problem to find that a library has cancelled its subscription because of financial constraints so that recent issues are not available. In such cases, alternative locations will have to be found and recorded. A similar problem may arise with CD-ROM and online databases, many of which do not go back more than a few years, though the printed equivalent may do so.

3. *The search terms to be used with that source* Recording search terms will ensure that each issue of the source will be searched in a consistent manner and that no search term is omitted. Some sources, for example *Chemical Abstracts*, review indexing terms every few years and there may be significant alterations in the vocabulary used. In such cases, a note of which terms to use for which dates is extremely useful.

4. *The volumes/issues that have been searched*

5. *The volumes/issues that remain to be searched*

6. *Online searches* These require a note of the databases used and a note of the (complete) search strategy that produced the final results.

7. *Internet searches* Likewise, these should be recorded with the full search strategy and the search engine(s) employed.

Some people also like to keep a count of how many useful items have turned up in each source, thus allowing them to identify the most fruitful titles. This can be very interesting but is not essential information. Indeed, some care has to be taken not to read too much into this sort of information because quantity and quality of references do not necessarily coincide.

The record of the search is most convenient when kept either on record cards or an A4 sheet of paper that can be kept in a ring binder and taken with the searcher. Such records may be created or updated on the spot as the search progresses and then no further work is required. A discussion of the merits and demerits of these two formats is given later. In this case, the record sheet is probably most convenient, as it has the advantage of displaying the entire picture of progress at a glance (see Table 6.1).

Table 6.1   Example of record of search progress

Sources	Search terms	Progress
British Humanities Index 1990 –	*Cruelty to children* *Children. Battered*	*1990, 91, 92, 93, 94, 95, 96, 97, 98, 99 except from April–*
Psychological Abstracts 1990–*	*Battered child* *Child abuse* *Family violence*	*1990, 91, 92, 93, 94, 95, 96, 97, 98, 99*
P.A.I.S. 1994–	*Child abuse*	*1994, 95, 96, 97, 98, 99*
Social Services Index 1990–	*Child abuse*	*1990, 91, 92, 93, 94, 95–98 at binding, due back May 99 Jan – April done*
Social Services Abstracts 1990–	*Child abuse*	*1990, 91, 92, 93, 94, 95, 96, 97, 98 except April issue missing. 99*

Recording the references found

It should hardly be necessary to point out that proper records should be kept of all likely references discovered during the course of a literature search, yet this obvious requirement is often overlooked. There have been many students, for example, who, while preparing the bibliography during the final stages of their thesis, have found that the references for several key documents have mysteriously vanished or are incomplete. Moreover, any memory of where these references had been discovered has long since evaporated – after all, the search may have been performed some months before. To be faced with the prospect of going through even part of the literature search again is extremely daunting, especially when the submission date for the completed work is looming closer and closer. If full records are kept this problem should not occur, nor should there ever be confusion between different items, even if the titles are very similar as often happens with a very specific topic, particularly when one or two authors dominate the field. In addition, all necessary details will be available for purposes such as looking the item up in a library catalogue, ordering it on inter-library loan, or consulting a librarian or supervisor with some query.

The information that should be kept about every reference found is as follows:

1. *The complete bibliographic reference* The writing of references is discussed in Chapter 8. The main thing to remember is to be consistent in the use of one method. In the course of any search it will be found that the form of reference will vary from source to source, which can be a little confusing. Rather than copy exactly what is found, it is a better idea to rewrite each reference into a standard format as the record is made (see Figure 6.1).

2. *The source where the reference was found* Give full details. Just putting a title is not very helpful, especially if the source is something the size of *Chemical Abstracts*. Give the year, volume number and the abstract number or subject heading as appropriate. This information is useful in cases where there is subsequently some difficulty in locating the item and it is necessary to check the details of the reference. Many inter-library loan services will automatically ask for the source details of every requested item for this reason. It does sometimes happen that there has been an error in copying a reference and this information will enable a correction to be made quickly. Alternatively, the original source may occasionally be incorrect, in which case it will be necessary to cross-check somewhere else.

3. *Location and availability* If a number of libraries are being used, then a reminder of where each reference may be seen, together with its shelf number, can be made. If the item has had to be reserved or ordered on inter-library loan, a note to this effect may be made with an indication of when it is likely

Butcher, David

Official information for business and industry. Refer 13(2). 1997. pp2-8

Source LISA 1998
Location Per 020

official info
govt info
business info

Front

This provides an overview of the relationship between business and government and of the relevance of official information to business and industry. Written since the privatization of TSO. Covers EU initiatives as well as British.

Back

Figure 6.1   Example of record card

to become available. Inter-library loan requests will cost the library about £10 to £15 a time, and they view duplicate requests, or failure to collect because the reader has forgotten about it, with a jaundiced eye. In fact this is one of the reasons why many libraries now charge for this service. If a collection of photocopies is made, cross-references to this may be made from the corresponding records.

4. *Whether the item has been read*   Possession of a copy of a reference often gives a comfortable feeling of achievement, as if possession equates with actual perusal of the item. As the

references accumulate, it is surprisingly easy to forget what has and has not been read.

5. *Annotation or abstract* It may be useful to indicate very briefly the content or particular importance of some or all of the references. If systematic notes have been made elsewhere, though, then there is little point in duplicating effort and a cross-reference to these notes could be made instead.

All this information may be recorded very easily and quickly. An example of such a record is illustrated, but there are many different ways of making the various notes. The important thing is to put specific information in the same position on each record so that it can be picked out quickly. Use of coloured and highlighting pens can also increase the ease with which the record is read.

Cards versus computers

There are many formats for keeping records of the type discussed above and the final choice must depend on factors such as the information that needs to be recorded, the number of records, and the manner in which the records need to be accessed. One of the most convenient ways is to use record cards, but many people prefer to use a computer database. A computer is a powerful tool and its great advantage is that it can store and manipulate large quantities of data very quickly. However, it should be pointed out that the number of records likely to be created as the result of a literature search for a dissertation or thesis is not going to be particularly large. This means that the great advantage of using computers is not going to be properly exploited. If there are only one or two hundred references on a file, then the time taken to log on, call up the database, recall a record, scan it, amend it, store it, close the file and log off will be considerably longer than if the same amendment was made manually on an equivalent card file. Even if, as is now normal practice, the end report or dissertation is going to be word-processed and the bibliography will therefore also be keyed in eventually, it is often much easier to leave this until the end. Using even a simple database can be more bother than it is worth for a small number of records, and there should be very positive reasons for deciding to use one. These reasons should be based on those characteristics of computers with which a manual system cannot compete; for example, using a computer might be best if:

● the database is going to be very large;
● the records will require frequent, highly sophisticated manipulation that cannot conveniently be done manually;
● much of the literature search is done electronically and data for the bibliographies can be downloaded and copied across to the text file. However, this is still not necessarily the quickest or most convenient method as most citations will need to be heavily edited before they can be used. Also, it is very difficult to reference from the text without having a print/manual list to work from;
● if the searcher owns a laptop that can be taken around when the search is being performed, though again a card system can still be handier at this stage of a search.

The disadvantages of using a computer database should be clearly understood. Unfortunately, for a novice, these may not become apparent until a commitment has been made to this form of record-keeping. Some of the main problems are as follows:

1. The location and access times of the terminals may be rather restricting and may not match personal work preferences. Apart from laptops or palmtops, a terminal is not portable and it is unlikely that the searcher will have access to it during the search process. Unless data is being downloaded, most of it will need to be transcribed twice, once from the original source and once from notes to the keyboard. This is time-consuming and is likely to lead to an increase in the number of errors. In addition, it is easy to forget or delay the updating of the database, which considerably lessens its usefulness.

2. The searcher will have to depend on printouts when searching to check for duplicates, etc. Even if the database is kept scrupulously up to date, the need to renew printouts after every update is time-consuming.

3. It is difficult to browse on a computer database, as normally only one record is displayed at a time. It is therefore difficult to compare records without having to make a printout.

4.   It is possible to crash a file and lose all the data, so time must be taken to make back-up copies after every update.
5.   The database may not allow the desired manipulation of the records. It can happen that the searcher may not be able to tell in advance of seeing the results of the search how best to use them.

If the decision is made to compile a computer database on either a mainframe or personal computer then there are many packages available that will accept and organize the sort of data being discussed. Such packages will usually provide search and retrieval facilities for author and subject headings at least (some will retrieve on any field of the record) and the file itself can be sorted and resorted according to different fields. Alternatively, it is possible to write a program from scratch, but this supposes that the researcher has both the time and the expertise to do so.

Most researchers are going to be restricted to the hardware and software available within their own organization. Even so, the types of software package required are sufficiently common to ensure that a choice is usually available and it is worth making some effort to find out exactly what there is. The computer centre may have a central register of software held throughout the institution. If not, it will be necessary to approach the library and any departments and individuals rumoured to use computers for a similar purpose. It is important to see, and especially to use, as many different packages as possible before deciding which one to adopt. No decision should be made in a hurry. Most packages tend to appear impressive on first sight, because a demonstration shows what they can do and not what they cannot. It is useful to take a checklist of all the functions that would be desirable to any demonstration and ask particularly about those functions not demonstrated.

There are a great number of books available on personal computers and the record systems that may be used on them. Unfortunately, the technology is developing so rapidly that publications become dated very soon after publication. There is a useful book by Heeks (1) that is specifically concerned with the creation of databases for recording bibliographic information for researchers rather than librarians. It is now somewhat old but is still in print.

When searching print sources, keeping records on a card

system is very convenient and has a number of advantages over a computer database. In the first place, a small file (up to two or even three hundred cards) is easily portable and can accompany the searcher at every stage of the search. This will allow instant checking for duplicate findings and, if a reference is new, then a record card can be written out on the spot and the file is instantly up to date. Amendments are equally easy to make.

Access to an individual card takes very little time with a file of this size. Even if the cards become a little dog-eared with use, access can be as fast or even faster than a computer, especially if guide cards are used. Card files are also very flexible. It is easy to change the order in which the records are arranged to suit the current needs of the research project. For example, while the literature search is in progress, cards may be kept in order of author for easy checking. Before writing begins, a reshuffle into subject order could indicate if there is a significant imbalance in the number of references obtained on different aspects of the subject. Once writing has commenced, the references for each chapter can be kept together, which will help to prevent any item being overlooked. Finally, the bibliography can be typed directly from the cards, which merely have to be arranged in the desired order. At any time, browsing through the file is very easy and it is possible to see and compare several cards simultaneously. These activities are not nearly so easy to accomplish with a computer record.

The recommended size of record card is A6 or 148 × 105 mm (6 in. by 4 in.) as this gives more room for making notes than the traditional library size of A7 or 105 × 74 mm (5 in. by 3 in.). Either size may be obtained in both ruled and plain format from most stationers. The cards may be kept in purpose-made plastic or cardboard filing boxes, which are well worth the modest investment required. A home-made receptacle such as a converted shoe box is generally less robust and, if lidless, less portable and more prone to accidental spillage. A simple rubber band round the cards is the cheapest method of keeping them together, but it is not so easy to flick through the cards and they tend to get much more grubby and worn.

One side of the card should contain the complete reference, together with a note of where the reference was found, two or three keywords and the location of the item. Any other information should be put on the back of the card. The front should not be too cluttered, as this makes it more difficult to pick out information quickly. In addition, any one piece of information should be placed in the same position on the card, as this enables it to be picked out much more easily when flicking through. If the location is sometimes at the top, sometimes at the bottom, or variously on the front and back of the cards, it means that each record has to be very carefully read to find the desired piece of information.

A number of other card systems have been devised in the past for personal files, such as edge-notched or optical coincidence (peek-a-boo) cards. These had a considerable vogue at one time but now are quite out of fashion because they do not show any real advantage over the system described above. Such extra subject retrieval ability as they did show has long been superseded by computer packages. However, the necessary cards can still be obtained from specialist suppliers, although they are quite expensive. Any reader who wishes more information on these methods of record-keeping is recommended to read the book by Foskett (2) if obtainable – it is now out of print but may still be found in specialist collections.

Records can, of course, also be kept on A4 sheets in a loose-leaf binder and students may well feel that this is more convenient in that all work can be kept together in the one file. Such sheets have many of the advantage of cards but they are not as easy to rearrange or to browse through as are cards. In addition, they are not as robust and, being considerably larger than cards, they are not so convenient to spread out for purposes of comparison.

Record-keeping methods may be used for all types of personal documentation. Unfortunately, the now widespread use of computers has led to other methods of record-keeping to be neglected even though they still have much to offer. There is no up-to-date literature on the topic but a book by Stibic (3) discusses the topic thoroughly, offering many other suggestions. However, it is worth repeating that the system used should be as simple as possible or the whole process can become tedious and time-consuming.

Organizing photocopies

Inevitably, a large number of photocopies will be obtained as a result of any literature search and it makes sense to cross-reference these with the records made. The simplest thing to do is to number each photocopy as it arrives and file them in that order. The location entry on the matching record can then give that number as the cross-reference. The advantage of this system is that it is quick and easy. There is little point in trying to organize the photocopies in some complicated subject order. Inevitably, some will cover two or more subjects and a decision has to be made as to which to ignore. The job of indexing in this way should be done by the record file not by the collection itself. Alternatively, the photocopies can be arranged in alphabetical order by author or even title, but it will be found that more care needs to be taken to file them in their correct places, whereas numerical filing by a number marked very clearly in some bright colour takes much less effort.

References

1. HEEKS, R., *Personal Bibliographical Indexes and Their Computerisation.* London, Taylor & Graham, 1988.

2. FOSKETT, A.C., *A Guide to Personal Indexes Using Edge-notched, Uniterm and Peek-a-boo Cards.* 2nd edn. London, Bingley, 1970, 91 pp. (out of print).

3. STIBIC, V., *Personal Documentation for Professionals: Means and Methods.* Amsterdam, North-Holland, 1980, 214 pp. (out of print).

7

Obtaining and evaluating the material

As the search progresses and relevant references are identified, the searcher will wish to get hold of the material in order to read it. A number of the references will be found in the home library and these will naturally be obtained and read first of all. It is very likely, however, that the majority of the references will not be so easily obtained. In this case the researcher normally has two choices. Either the items are located in other libraries that are then visited in person, or the home library is asked to obtain the required items from another library via the inter-library loan network.

Locating and visiting other libraries

How practical this course of action will be will depend very much on the degree of proximity of other libraries and the amount of useful material that they hold. In the larger cities there may well be one or more universities, colleges of further education and a sizeable public reference library, all providing collections that can be called upon. Cities such as London, Birmingham, Leeds,

Oxford, Cambridge, Edinburgh or Glasgow will have excellent resources and a short visit of a few days will be well rewarded. If a number of references can be located in one library or several libraries that are near to each other, then it is worth travelling some distance to spend a day or two of concentrated effort. The protocol to be observed in visiting other libraries has been discussed in Chapter 1.

Union catalogues

The first problem is to locate the desired items, and the most important tools for this task are the union catalogues. Most of the larger libraries in this country now belong to one of the regional or national co-operative cataloguing schemes, whereby the cataloguing for each of the member libraries is done centrally. This is done primarily for economic reasons and the cataloguing data is held on a computer database. The catalogues in the member libraries may be online but there is often a microfiche copy as back-up. An example of a national co-operative scheme used by many academic libraries is TALIS, formerly BLCMP (Birmingham Libraries Co-operative Mechanisation Project). Two other major schemes are SWALCAP (South West Academic Libraries Co-operative Automation Project) and SCOLCAP (Scottish Libraries Co-operative Automation Project).

One of the products of such centralized cataloguing systems is a 'union catalogue', which is a joint catalogue of the collections of all the participating libraries. The union catalogue is often produced on microfiche and usually each library will have at least one copy of this. Alternatively, online access may be provided, often through the SuperJANET network. The union catalogue will include books, journals and other serials, audio-visual material and music. It is arranged like any other catalogue, and when an item is found it will be seen that the entry is followed by a number of alphabetical codings. Each code identifies a co-operating library that holds a copy of the item in question. Alongside the catalogue there should be a list of the codes used, together with the full names of the libraries so identified.

There are some old printed union catalogues available, such as the *British Union Catalogue of Periodicals (BUCOP)*. The basic work, consisting of four volumes, was published in 1958, since when various forms of supplement have been produced, including the *BUCOP Journal*, although it has now ceased publication. The task of producing printed union lists is now rarely an economic one and they are usually computerized.

Library catalogues

Some libraries print catalogues of their own holdings and copies of these are to be found in many academic libraries. An example is the *London Bibliography of the Social Sciences* (1), which is basically the catalogue of the British Library of Political and Economic Science, though it does include entries for items held in some other libraries. Again, this activity is largely superseded by networked systems such as that described below.

SuperJANET

JANET stands for Joint Academic Network. The original JANET was developed back in the 1980s as a telecommunications network that links the universities in the United Kingdom as well as research councils, many further education colleges, some commercial organizations and other national bodies which range from the British Library to some of the major charitable research bodies. Among the various facilities it offers, it allows a subscriber to access the online public-access catalogue (OPAC) of a specific member library and search it directly. It is therefore an extremely useful tool for locating materials. The system was upgraded to SuperJANET and in 1993 the Superjournal project was initiated to take advantage of the new high-speed network. This project involved nine publishers, including Blackwell Scientific Publications, Macmillan and Oxford University Press, and offers online versions of a number of journal titles, incorporating graphics as well as text. This allows speedy document delivery to subscribers.

Inter-library loans

All libraries will provide this service to their users and very often it is provided free of charge. However, it is becoming more common for some sort of fee to be charged, as it is an expensive service to provide. It has been estimated that the cost of obtaining a single item is about £10 to £15, including the cost of an inter-library loan (ILL) voucher and administration costs. In some academic libraries an applicant will be restricted in the number of ILL requests that can be made in a certain period, or charged for each one. If this is so then a good deal of thought must be given concerning the selection of items to be obtained in this manner, so that the most useful ones are requested first. This will require the references found during the search to be arranged in some order of priority. To do this, the searcher will have to have completed a fair proportion of the search before ILL requests are made.

Many libraries automatically send all ILL requests to the British Library Document Supply Centre (DSC) at Boston Spa in Yorkshire, which was set up specifically to be a national lending library. The DSC's prime function is to acquire as complete a collection of the world's literature as is possible and to make this material available for loan to other libraries. It has built up enormous collections of non-fiction books (some five million), journals (some 62 000 current titles), which are listed in *Serials in the British Library* (2), reports, conference literature, microforms, theses and translations of all types of material. The materials come from all countries and all subjects are covered. Further information may be obtained from the British Library's Web site (3), which also allows free searching of all its catalogues. The DSC lends only to libraries, not to individuals, and the material may be provided in the form of a photocopy or microfiche that can be retained by the requester, or an original copy is provided that must be returned in due course.

It is estimated that over 80 per cent of all ILL requests in this country are satisfied by the DSC. If the item is in stock then the request will be supplied within a week or ten days of the request being made at the home library. (The turnaround time at the DSC itself is usually not more than a couple of days; most of the delay is due to processing procedures at the home library and to the postal service.) If the item is out on loan then there will obviously be a greater delay, especially if the item is in some demand and there is a queue of requesters waiting to see it. If by any chance the DSC does not have the item requested, it will forward the request to other libraries in the ILL network, and in this case there again may be a considerable delay before the item is provided. In order to make an ILL request, the searcher must fill out a form at the home library for each item required. Complete details should be given, including the source of the reference, in order to minimize the possibility of confusion in identifying the item.

Some libraries belong to a local or regional ILL network. Often this is based on the co-operative cataloguing scheme to which the library belongs and any item appearing in the union catalogue will be borrowed locally rather than from the DSC. This is often a much cheaper procedure for the participating libraries and the more efficient networks can be amazingly fast. If an item is required urgently, then the arrangements can be made by phone and the item can be faxed or delivered next day. Not all local ILL networks are as fast, however, and it may be better to visit the library holding the item unless the searcher needs to study it over a number of days. Increasingly, as libraries are networked, it is becoming possible to obtain electronic delivery of documents.

Translations

Some researchers may find that some really interesting items discovered during the literature search have been published in a foreign language. The entry in the bibliography, indexing or abstracting journal will indicate if this is so, though the indication is often a very brief one, such as (Fr) or (Jap) at the end of the entry, which can very easily be overlooked. It would be very unfortunate if valuable material is not used merely because it is written in a different language and there are various avenues of approach to this problem that can be explored.

The DSC holds a very large number of translations of documents of all kinds, particularly journal articles. If an ILL request is clearly marked 'English translation required' then a search will be made to see if such a translation has been made. About 25 per cent of such requests are satisfied, but if a translation cannot be provided by the DSC then it is worth applying to Aslib, who maintain a register of over half a million translated items. This index is a location list only and the enquirer will be put in touch with the organization that holds the required item.

A number of journals, particularly Russian, Japanese and Chinese, are translated in full and re-published as English language journals a few months after the publication of the original. These are known as cover-to-cover translations and the titles treated in this way are listed in *Journals in Translation* (4), published by the British Library.

Many professional librarians in academic libraries have a good working knowledge of a language and will be able to sit down with the researcher and give a rough indication as to the contents of an article. Often this is enough to identify the required information or at least make it clear whether a full translation is essential or not.

It is possible, as a last resort, to commission a translation, but this may be difficult to organize, especially if it is required in a hurry. It will be necessary to find a translator who not only knows the language well, but the subject area also, especially if it is a technical one. Translation is not just a matter of mechanical word matching, and grave errors can be made if the subject matter is not understood. There are various national registers of translators available, such as those maintained by Aslib or the Institute of Linguists, or the library may have a list of local people who are prepared to do this sort of work.

Commissioning a translation is expensive. Translations of the more difficult or unusual languages may cost £60 to £80 per page. If the subject is also a difficult one then the cost may soar to well over £100 per page. It is therefore not a transaction to be entered upon lightly, and it is very important to make absolutely sure that a translation is not already in existence before one is commissioned.

Copying and copyright

Many items requested through the ILL system will be provided in the form of a photocopy that may be retained by the user, but it will frequently happen that researchers will wish to make their own copies from the original. This is an area with a number of pitfalls for the unwary and may prove a source of friction between library and researcher if it appears that the Copyright Act is being breached.

A new copyright law came into force in 1996 that has made a number of changes over the previous legislation, though these are likely to affect libraries more than the individual researcher. Most libraries now participate in the Copyright Licensing Agreement (CLA) and must abide by its conditions. These allow copying from publications that fall under the terms of the agreement but, unfortunately, there are a number of publishers and categories of work that are excluded from the terms of the CLA licence, as are works published in certain non-participating countries. Permission must be obtained from the publisher before copying from any of these. There is a list of works excluded from the CLA and participating libraries will have these for reference, often posted near the photocopier. Generally speaking it is still permissible for a person to make one copy of a journal article, providing it is going to be used for personal research only and a declaration is signed to this effect. The method of copying does not matter, the declaration must be signed even if the copying is done by hand, a fact that most people do not realize. Multiple copies must not be made, nor may a copy be sold or used for other purposes than research unless permission to do so has been obtained in writing from the copyright holder. This may be either the author or the publisher of the work in question.

When a researcher wishes to make copies of categories of material other than books or journals, the copyright position may be a good deal more complicated. Some material may not be copied at all without written permission from the copyright holders. Such documents will have printed in them a statement to this effect, generally on the inside of the cover or on the back of the title page. Yet other documents will be found to have a statement indicating that they can be freely copied without such permission. This is often true of electronic documents, especially on private sites on the Web, although the author may ask for certain conditions to be met, such as acknowledging the original source. Any material obtained should be carefully examined for such statements; if none are found then it may be assumed that it falls under the general copyright rules indicated above. The exception is unpublished material (including theses), which is fully protected; and no copying should be done without the author's permission.

There is much abuse of copyright due to the wide availability of photocopiers, widespread ignorance of copyright law and the difficulty of detecting lawbreakers and bringing a prosecution. Indeed the new Copyright Act has partly resulted from widespread concern about the abuse of the system and it behoves every researcher to treat other authors' works in the manner that he or she would wish their own to be treated. It should also be remembered that if widespread abuses are found to occur within a particular library, it is likely that it will suffer penalties that will affect every user of that library.

Evaluating material

All researchers should develop their evaluative skills when coping with the results of a literature search. It very often happens that the results of a full search can be overwhelming in the sheer quantity of material identified, to the extent that it is just not possible to deal thoroughly with it all in the time available. Apart from this, it can also become an expensive business to obtain large quantities of material. The researcher must therefore consider ways and means by which the material can be controlled. There are, of course, simple but undiscriminating methods of reducing a large amount of material, such as using only material of a certain age or by discarding foreign language items or by omitting certain categories of material. As discussed elsewhere in this book, all these methods should only be considered as a last resort, as they all carry the risk of discarding material of key importance. If it appears at an early stage in the search that the amount of material is going to be overwhelming, then it would be a good idea to look again at the topic of the search and focus on that instead. It may be possible to break a larger search down into smaller topic searches which will help the researcher to maintain control over the material.

Rather than discard material before it has even been seen, the application of evaluative skills can assist the searcher to identify the most important and relevant items. Evaluative skills should be used at two stages, first to decide which references should be obtained and second, once the material is at hand, to decide whether it is of core interest, of minor importance or, after all, not relevant to the topic.

The former task is the more difficult because in many indexes and bibliographies only minimum information is given. It may often be necessary to make a decision based on the title alone, although, with experience, the author's name or the journal in which an article is published may suggest a certain usefulness or otherwise to the searcher. If an abstract is given then this should supply sufficient information to indicate the usefulness of the item, although even quite lengthy abstracts can be misleading in that not every aspect of the article can be covered. At this stage of the search then, the evaluation has to be based upon such information as:

- the author(s), his or her qualifications, and knowledge of other articles written by him or her, particularly important when evaluating Web sites, some of which are highly unreliable;
- the institution where the work was carried out;
- the title;
- the abstract, if any;
- the subject indexing of the source being used. (Look at other items under the same headings. Does the indexing seem consistent? Is it specific or rather general?)

It is a good idea to collect a fairly large number of references before making demands upon the inter-library loan service or visiting other libraries. If this is done the accumulation of references will soon begin to give extra information, such as the journal titles which appear to be the most important publishers in the required subject, the names of the authors who are most active, or the institutions where most research on the topic has been carried out. All this information together will begin to give the searcher a 'feel' for the literature of the subject. As the references accumulate, a decision must be made as to the apparent importance of each item so that they can be arranged in order of priority. This will then determine, to a large extent, the order in which the items are obtained and read. It is particularly necessary to do this if there are any restrictions on the number of inter-library loans that one individual may request.

When copies of the references are obtained, it is necessary to confirm the importance of each, so that some sort of priority for proper reading may be made. This is particularly important when there is a good deal of material or a restricted amount of time available for reading. It may well be that some of the references turn out to be much less important than first thought. In fact it is almost inevitable that this should be so, given the sparse information on which some of the initial evaluations will have been made. It is therefore helpful to acquire the art of scanning material very quickly in order to obtain a general impression of its usefulness. Time can be wasted by reading carefully through papers that in the end turn out to be of little value.

Scanning

This process involves looking only at the more significant features of an item, which may include the following:

1. *Abstract or author's summary*   It is becoming quite usual to include a summary at the head of an article or report, though occasionally it may appear at the end rather than the beginning.
2. *Introductory paragraphs*   These should make clear the subject of the article, the approach the author is taking and the particular aspects that will be dealt with.
3. *Concluding paragraphs*   These will often summarize the most important points.
4. *Illustrative material*   This may include, among other things, tables, graphs, charts, diagrams and photographs. Often, if specific information is required, it can be picked straight from such features without the need to read much text. In such a case, it should also be remembered that the language barrier is transcended by this sort of visual presentation and a translation may not, after all, be essential. Many abstracting and indexing journals will indicate if an article has illustrative material for this reason.

5. *Section or paragraph headings* These will usually indicate the main topics within the article and the progression of the argument. They can in their own right be very informative, especially in reports, which are generally given to using them far more than other categories of material.

The whole scanning process should only take four or five minutes and the documents can then be sorted according to their importance to give the order in which they should be read with more attention. Irrelevant material may be set aside or returned at once to the library from whence it came.

It is helpful to purchase or build up a collection of photocopies of the core material (with due regard for the copyright laws) as it may be necessary to refer to some material again and again during the course of a research project. It will then be possible to mark significant passages with highlighter pens or similar means as required, something that definitely should not be done with other people's property. Rather than make photocopies of material of minor importance, it is better and cheaper to note the significant points that are offered on the back of the record card (see Chapter 6).

References

1. *London Bibliography of the Social Sciences* (British Library of Political and Economic Science). London, Mansell Publ., 1931–. Annual.

2. *Serials in the British Library; together with locations and holdings of other British and Irish libraries.* London, British Library Bibliographic Services, 1981–. Quarterly, with a rolling annual cumulation on microfiche. Also available on the DSC Web site.

3. www.bl.uk/services/bsds

4. *Journals in Translation.* 4th edn. Boston Spa, British Library Document Supply Centre, 1988.

8

Writing references

When a relevant item is found during a literature search, the details that are noted are collectively known as the *bibliographic reference* or the *bibliographic citation*. The function of the bibliographic reference is to allow a reader to identify the item easily and clearly with no possibility of confusing it with another work. Thus it should be clear from the reference what format is involved, whether it is a book, journal article, thesis, web page, and so on, and the details necessary to locate the precise part of the work that is being referred to. A citation should not be confused with the more detailed descriptions found in a library catalogue or some of the commercial bibliographies. These have a somewhat different function and there is no need to become involved in the intricacies of formal cataloguing. The bibliographic references should be restricted to the essential information only.

The writing of references often causes a considerable amount of difficulty and confusion. This is partly because there are so many acceptable ways in which they can be written and any sizeable literature search will turn up half a dozen different styles. Confusion has also arisen because of the heavy use of electronic sources in literature searching and the difficulties in deciding how to cite the material found in these. It is understandable that the easiest course of action is to copy down the references exactly as they are found during the search, but this will result in a muddled and inconsistent bibliography. Ideally, one acceptable method of writing references should be chosen and thoroughly understood before any records have to be made. Then, when a suitable reference is found, it can be immediately 'translated' into the chosen style as the record is made. If this is done consistently then the record file will be more easily organized. Moreover, the lists of references and bibliography can be typed up directly from the records with no need for further alteration. In all, a great deal of time will be saved.

Some researchers may find that they have no choice regarding the method that they use. Quite a number of institutions require a particular style to be adopted and it is advisable to find out what the position is as soon as possible. Many academic institutions prefer the Harvard system, for example, while authors writing books or journal articles will find that publishers will often have their own differing house styles. Usually authors will be sent appropriate instructions or, in the case of journals, such information is often available in every issue. It is as well to check before any writing is done.

A comparison of the different methods of writing references will show that the variations occur more as differences in the order and style in which the information is given than in the information itself. This is because for any one type of reference, for example a book or journal article, the essential information required for identification is always going to be the same. Once this is understood, the whole process becomes a lot easier. The method described here is recommended because it is one of the simplest and clearest. It is closely based upon the recommendations given in British Standard 1629 (1), which is equivalent to the International Standard ISO 690 (2). To discover acceptable alternatives, it is only necessary to look at half a dozen reputable journals and study the lists of references at the ends of the articles.

Initially, references will be taken from the bibliographic source that is being searched, and the searcher will therefore be dependent on that source for the details required. However, all the references used will have (or certainly should have) been read, which means that a copy or photocopy will be seen at some time. It is always worth checking the details of the reference with the copy obtained. Missing details can then be filled in or mistakes in the source, which not infrequently occur, can be corrected. In describing the various problems that can occur in writing references, therefore, it has been assumed that a copy will be seen. Another point that should be made is that it is now commonplace to find a reference to a print item on an electronic source such as the Internet, CD-ROM or online host. In such cases, the print source is the original and the reference should be given as standard, although it is quite helpful to give a Web address at the end.

The basic rule about any reference is that the information given should always answer certain questions about the item:

- *who* is it by?
- *what* is it called?
- *how, when and where* was it published?

In addition, care should be taken that all references are:

- *correct* – in respect to every detail included;
- *complete* – all essential information is given;
- *consistent* – in the way they are written.

Book references

The information required to identify a book reference includes:

- author or editor;
- title;
- edition (other than first);
- place of publication;
- publisher;
- date of publication;
- number of pages (optional).

The straightforward book reference will therefore look like this:

MOORE, N., *How to do Research*. 2nd edn. London, Library Association, 1987, 150 pp.

TRIPPENSEE, R.E., *Wildlife Management*. New York, McGraw-Hill, 1948, 1953, 2 vols

The elements of the reference are given in this order because it reflects the sequence in which the information is required if the item is looked up in a catalogue or index. The problem is that so many books are not as straightforward as this and all sorts of awkward little problems may occur. Some of the commoner variations are discussed below.

Author

Capital letters are helpful to make the name stand out clearly and to distinguish it from the title, which could also be a person's name. The surname is given first, followed by the initials or full forename if this is known. If there are two authors, then both should be given:

COWDREY, B. and SMITH, L.

If there are more than two authors, then the first named only is given, followed by et al. (Latin *'et alii'* meaning 'and others' to indicate that it is not a sole authorship).

BEVERLEY, C. et al.

Sometimes a book may have editors rather than authors. In these cases exactly the same rules are followed, with the addition of (ed.) or (eds) after the name(s).

COKER, T. (ed.)
LATTIMER, L. and SOLMON, T. (eds)
COLES, T. et al. (eds)

Occasionally, a book may have both an author and an editor, as for example when a classic literary work is reissued with a commentary. In such cases, the author, as being responsible for the main work, should be preferred. If it is felt that the editor is sufficiently important to be noted, then this name will come after the title.

BRONTE, CHARLOTTE, *Jane Eyre*. Edited by O.D. Leavis. Harmondsworth, Penguin, 1966.

In these cases it is usually not necessary to put in the editor as well, unless the text is specifically referring to their contribution to the work. Similarly, if translators or illustrators are important, they may be treated the same way, using 'translated by' or 'illustrated by' as appropriate if it is considered that their contribution is particularly important.

Remember that an author need not be an individual. It could be an industrial firm, a research association, a society, an institute or any other corporate body. If it appears that a book has no author, check again for an institutional responsibility. Treat corporate authors in the same way as personal authors. Very often, a corporate author will also be the publisher, in which case the name will have to appear twice in the reference. Another common occurrence is the book with a corporate author and individual editors. The editors are given after the title as in the example below.

INSTITUTE OF BANKERS, *Management and People in Banking*. Edited by B.L. Livy. 2nd edn. London, Institute of Bankers, 1987.
READERS' DIGEST, *Book of Facts*. London, Readers' Digest Association, 1985.

Occasionally a book will genuinely show no attributable author, editor or other responsible body. Such items can be attributed to 'Anon', but it is often more useful to list them under the title instead, especially if there are a great number of them in the bibliography.

Evaluation of National Performance in Basic Research. London, Royal Society Policy Studies Unit, 1986.

Title

The only real problem that tends to occur is with the sub-title. Subtitles can be extremely valuable, especially if the main title is rather cryptic. '*Help*' by itself is not very informative, but '*Help; the story of a teenage glue sniffer*' is much more useful. The rule

therefore should be to include the sub-title whenever it con-
tributes useful information. Very occasionally a sub-title or even a
title can be of an extraordinary and excessive length. If it is going
to take up more than about four or five lines of type, and if there is
a convenient break point, then it is permissible to put the first part
only and follow this with three dots to indicate that part of the
sub-title has been omitted. It is sometimes better to give the beginning and end of a sub-title and leave out the middle part. The need
to do this occurs only rarely, though, and it should not be looked
upon as a convenient way to avoid preparing references properly.

Full title:

Heraldry in miniature containing all the arms, crests, supporters
and mottoes of the peers, peeresses and bishops of England,
Scotland and Ireland with the Baronets of Great Britain and the
insignia of the different orders of knighthood in the three King-
doms.

Shortened title:

Heraldry in miniature . . .

Sometimes a multi-volume work will have different sub-titles for
each volume. If the entire work is being referred to, these can be
left out, but if only one volume is referred to then the sub-title may
be included after the volume number.

TRIPPENSEE, R.E., *Wildlife Management.* New York, McGraw-
Hill, 1953, Vol. 2: Fur bearers, waterfowl and fish, 572 pp.

An acceptable and in many ways preferable alternative is:

TRIPPENSEE, R.E., *Wildlife Management.* Vol. 2: Fur bearers,
waterfowl and fish, New York, McGraw-Hill, 1953, 572 pp.

Edition statement

This should always be given in figures, that is, '16th edn' not 'six-
teenth edn'. The first edition of a book traditionally is not given an

edition statement, only second and subsequent editions. Do not confuse editions with subsequent impressions or reprints. An edition consists of all copies made from the same set of type and later impressions are in fact part of that edition, even if they are made several years after. The publication history of a book will usually be found on the back of the title page, though nowadays it is not always given with the scrupulous detail of 50 years ago.

Place of publication

By place is meant town or city rather than country, though when there is a likelihood of confusion, for example when the town is London, Ontario, or when it is sufficiently obscure that most people will not know which country it is in, it is as well to make this clear. It is useful to give this information, as it indicates the national origins of the book (as merchandise) to intending purchasers. One cannot safely assume, however, corresponding national affiliations in the author. For example, many Australian authors have chosen to publish in this country, presumably to gain access to a wider market. The problem in writing references comes when a publisher has offices in two or more countries and lists them all on the title page. Sometimes the one required is clearly indicated by position or size of type, but this is not always so. To look for other indications can often increase confusion, as books may be printed in a different country from the one in which they are published, and American spelling may occur in a book published in England. Use the first place listed if there is no obvious reason to choose one of the others.

Publisher's name

It is necessary only to put down the essential part of the name. Such additions as '& Co.', '& Sons Ltd' may be safely omitted.

Methuen	not Methuen & Co.
Allen & Unwin	not George Allen & Unwin Ltd

Some well-known publishers are customarily referred to by their initials, OUP for Oxford University Press, for example. This is perfectly correct, but do make sure that it is an accepted initialism otherwise confusion could result. For example, the Open University Press should never be referred to as OUP. It is abbreviated to OU instead. If in doubt, spell it out.

Date of publication

This is the year in which the edition referred to was published. Ignore any subsequent impression dates. It is the date of the edition that dates the contents of the book. It could be very annoying to spend time obtaining what appears to be a recent book on a topic only to find that it is the 22nd impression of something originally published in 1962. The exception is when a book that has been long out of print is given a facsimile reprint. There are publishers that specialize in this type of work. In such a case both the original date and the reprint date can be given.

1932 (facsimile reprint 1987)

Do not use the copyright date unless no edition date is given; quite often the two are slightly different. If the copyright date is the only one to be found, a small © is used to indicate what it is.

© 1998

Pages

It is a matter of choice if this information is included or not. The person reading the reference may be interested to know whether the item is a 20-page pamphlet or a 700-page treatise. The number of pages (only those paginated in ordinary numerals are counted) may therefore be given at the end of the citation, unless a particular page or sequence of pages is being referred to, in which case the more specific information is given instead.

Referring to part of a book

It may be that a book consists of a series of articles or chapters by different authors and the reference is to one of these articles only. Such books will probably have an editor who may or may not have contributed to the text. In this case it is necessary to give what is in effect a double reference, with the more specific item coming first.

CLARK, A.S., Computer-assisted library instruction. IN J. Lubans (ed.), *Educating the Library User*. New York, Bowker, 1974, pp. 336–349.

The use of the word 'in' makes it clear what is happening. It might be argued that to give the reference as

LUBANS, J., *Educating the Library User*. New York, Bowker, 1974, pp. 336–349.

would be simpler and still lead the reader to the same information. However, this would not be acceptable as the true author is not being given the acknowledgement to which she is entitled. A reference should always be as specific as possible.

References to journal articles

The principle of answering *who, what, where* and *when* still applies, as it does for any reference. The information required for a journal article is:

- author(s);
- title of article;
- title of journal;
- volume, part or issue number;
- date;
- pages.

The reference will therefore look something like this:

TRIPATHI, V., John Pepper Clark – Nigerian poet and dramatist. *African Quarterly*, 16(4), April 1977, pp. 120–124.
McNEIL, R.I. et al., Isomerization of tetra-hydroaromatic groups under coal liquefaction conditions. *Fuel*, 62, April 1983, pp. 401–406.

The author and title of the article should be treated as described under book references.

Title of journal

This should be given in italic type to distinguish it from the title of the article or indeed any other part of the reference. Alternatively it could be printed in bold or underlined, but neither method looks quite so neat. Journal titles may be abbreviated but only to officially accepted abbreviations. The two main errors that occur are first, home-made abbreviations that no one can decipher, and second, one title being written in a number of different ways. Sometimes, the correct abbreviation is printed on the cover or title page of each issue of a journal. If not, there is a British Standard (BS 4148) (3) and an International Standard (ISO 4) (4) which deal with this topic.

Volume and date

Journals variously display some or all of the following: volume numbers, part numbers, running issue numbers, month (or season, for example spring, fall) and year. Put down everything that can be found in the order listed above. The part number should immediately follow the volume number and be enclosed in parentheses: 6(4) means volume 6, part 4. There is no need to put 'vol.' or 'part' in words; however, it is helpful to differentiate a running issue number from the other numbers by using 'No.', for example No. 2443.

Very occasionally journals are issued with no identification of date or issue at all. This may be a deliberate policy so that the issue can be circulated over a long period of time without obviously becoming dated. In other instances it may be a case of ignorance on the part of an individual or small society who is publishing privately. Whatever the reason, it causes enormous difficulty when writing a bibliographic reference, but there is little that can be done. It may be possible to deduce the year of publication by looking for dates or events mentioned in the text, or the printer's imprint may be dated.

Pages

The inclusive page numbers for the article should be given. If an article is interrupted by advertisements or other features this can be indicated by showing all the page sequences, for example pp. 6–9, 14–19. It is essential that all sequences are noted otherwise it can easily happen that a request for a photocopy results in only part of the article being provided.

Conferences, congresses, seminars, etc.

These references seem to cause a great deal of trouble, both in recognizing them when they turn up in a bibliography and in writing them. Most references will be to a specific paper but it may also be necessary to refer to the entire proceedings. In the first case, the procedure is very similar to referring to a chapter of a book. The author's name is followed by the title of the paper. Then comes the word IN followed by the details of the conference or symposium. The inclusion of IN shows clearly that the paper referred to is only a part of the whole, and also helps to distinguish it from a journal article.

When referring to the conference, the rule is that if it has a name then this should be used as the 'author'. If it has no name, but is a meeting of an organization, then that organization is the author. If the conference meets neither of these criteria then it should be treated as if it was anonymous. In other words it is listed under the title. Other details that are useful to supply are the number of the conference if it is one of a numbered series, the place and date and the editor's name if this is given.

Examples of *name* entry:

BEIJING INTERNATIONAL SYMPOSIUM ON HYDROGEN SYSTEMS 1985. Hydrogen systems; proceedings of Beijing International Symposium, New York, Pergamon, 1986. 2 vols, 1136 pp.
DIVETECH 84, Developments in diving technology; proceedings of an international conference organized by the Society for

Underwater Technology, held London, 14–15 Nov. 1984, London, Graham & Trotman, 1985, 157 pp.

Example of *organization* entry:

SOCIETY FOR THE STUDY OF PATHOPHYSIOLOGY OF PREGNANCY-ORGANIZATION GESTOSIS. Actual standing in EPH-gestosis; proceedings of the 16th Congress of the Society..., held Aachen, 15–18 June, 1984, Amsterdam, *Excerpta Medica*, 1985, 487 pp.

Example of *title* entry:

The Euphorbiales; chemistry, taxonomy and economic botany, proceedings of a joint symposium organized by the Linnean Society of London and the Phytochemical Society of Europe, London, Academic Press, 1987, 325 pp.

There is often a good deal more information available about this type of publication, as may be seen by looking at a catalogue entry. However, the reference does not need any more detail than is indicated in the examples above. This is quite enough to identify the works clearly.

References to reports, theses, patents and standards

These follow the same general rules as have already been discussed.

Reports   Numbered technical reports should be treated in the same way as a book, but the report series and number should be included after the date.

SIMON, J.D., *Misperceiving the terrorist threat.* Santa Monica, Rand Corp., 1987. (Report No. RAND/R-3423-RC)
CENTRAL INTELLIGENCE AGENCY, *South Africa; political influence groups.* Springfield, Va N.T.I.S., 1988. (PB88-927905/GAR)

Unpublished theses As these will obviously have no publisher, the name of the institution awarding the degree is given instead, together with the type of degree for which the thesis was prepared, for example PhD or MSc.

COCKMAN, T.L., *West German rearmament, from enemy to ally in ten short years.* MSc. Thesis, Indiana University, 1988.

Patents The patent may be taken out by an individual but more often the patentee is an industrial company or similar institution. The 'author' is the one who has taken out the patent. The individual(s) may also be included in the reference if desired, and should be put after the title. It is very important when giving the patent specification number to indicate which country has given the patent.

UNION CARBIDE CORPORATION, *Improved tubular cellulosic food casing.* GB Patent Specification B1 584 435, 11th Feb. 1981.

Standards Again, these may be treated in the same manner as a book, but add the standard number after the date. This number should include the identification of the body which has compiled the standard, for example BS 2570, ISO 1532.

BRITISH STANDARDS INSTITUTION, *Specification for surface plates.* London, B.S.I., 1988. BS 817.

It is not possible to give examples for all the different types of publication that may occur and the variations that may occur within each type. However, if the basic principles of writing references are understood, and the various examples given above are studied carefully, then it should be a relatively easy matter to compile acceptable records.

References to electronic documents

Unfortunately the Standards referred to in this chapter have not got to grips with the problem of citing electronic documents, in particular Internet documents, though the problem is under consideration. The following advice is therefore based on the same principles as have already been discussed. The first point to establish is whether the original document is in electronic form or whether the electronic source is displaying a document that is a print original. This is increasingly a source of confusion as there are now many full text online databases, electronic journals and electronic versions of conference papers and other material. If the item being referred to has been published in print form then use the appropriate standard reference format discussed above. It should not be assumed that everyone has access to electronic sources. If it is wished, an annotation can then be made to the effect that the document may also be read at the appropriate electronic address.

If the document is only available in electronic form, and this will mostly apply to Internet documents, then the basic principles should still be followed. In other words, the author of the document, the title, the source and the date should be given wherever possible, as well as the Web address. Admittedly there does seem to be a trend to give the address only, but this is not very helpful to the user and it is a better policy to give as many of the standard elements as can be identified.

NATIONAL LIBRARY OF AUSTRALIA. National strategy for provision of access to Australian electronic publications; a NLA position paper. 18th Feb. 1998. (http://www.nla.gov.au/policy/paep.html)

OKERSON, A. The electronic journal; what, whence and when? *Public Access Computer Systems Review*, 2(1), 1991. (http://info.lib.uh.edu/pr/v2/n1/okerson.2nl)

References

1. BRITISH STANDARDS INSTITUTION, *Recommendations for Bibliographic References*. Milton Keynes, B.S.I., 1976 (BS 1629).

2. INTERNATIONAL STANDARDS ORGANIZATION, *Documentation Bibliographic References – Essential and Supplementary Elements*. Geneva, I.S.O., 1975 (ISO 690).

3. BRITISH STANDARDS INSTITUTION, *Specification for Abbreviation of Title Words and Titles of Publications*. Milton Keynes, B.S.I., 1985 (BS 4148).

4. INTERNATIONAL STANDARDS ORGANIZATION, *Documentation International Code for the Abbreviation of Titles of Periodicals*. Geneva, I.S.O., 1972 (ISO 4).

9

Citing references in the text

When the text of the dissertation or thesis is finally written, attention must be drawn to the material used in the course of its preparation. It is important to show that this material has in fact been read and taken account of in the subsequent research. It has happened that a pharmacy student performed a hasty and indiscriminate literature search after his thesis was written because his supervisor asked to see the bibliography. The effort was unconvincing, partly because the search missed most of the key references, partly because his most relevant reference turned out to be available only in Serbo-Croat, but largely because (not surprisingly) no mention had been made of *any* of the references in the text of the thesis.

There are various ways in which the results of the literature search may be incorporated into the text.

Review of the literature

In most dissertations and theses the inclusion of a review of the literature will be a requirement anyway, or even the theme, of the dissertation but, even if not specified, it is very good practice to include a short and critical review of work already published in the field. It sets the work in context and can also show very neatly how the rest of the thesis develops new lines of thought or discovery from existing knowledge. The work discussed must be central to the topic, however, and the student should be prepared for questions about this literature in any oral examination. The review of the literature should be put immediately after the introduction or the statement of the scope aims and purpose of the dissertation. A literature review may also be an integral part or even the main purpose of many types of publication including books, journal articles or reports.

It is outside the scope of this work to discuss how to go about writing such a review, but the topic has been covered in Hart's book (1), which, though centred on research in the social sciences, discusses all the general principles of analysing and mapping the arguments and ideas that appear in the literature and writing the review.

Lists of references

Specific sources of information and ideas, which refer readers to a full reference listed elsewhere, should always be given an acknowledgement in the text, usually at the end of the chapter. All published references mentioned in the text should be included but no other material should appear in these lists. The method of arrangement of a list of references will depend very much on the method of citation used in the text.

There are several methods by which references may be cited in the text and only a few, chosen for their relative simplicity, are described here. It is useful to refer to British Standard BS 5605 (2), which gives 'concise guidance for authors and editors on the preferred methods of arranging lists of references in books and journals articles. Includes methods of making attribution within the text'.

Footnotes

These are short notes, printed at the foot of a page, to which the attention of the reader is drawn by some signal in the main text, such as an asterisk or a superscript number. Readers of Terry Pratchett will be familiar with the system. Footnotes may consist of a citation or of explanatory material that is supplementary to the main discussion. They should be printed in a considerably smaller type than the text so that the two cannot be confused. Because of the trouble of doing this, whether in typescript, word processing or type setting, footnotes are now rarely used. It is a method that is not very convenient for the reader either, as the text becomes irregularly presented. In some nineteenth-century books (when footnotes were extensively used), there can be page after page containing more footnote than text. Citations for a particular chapter become separated from each other, so no picture of the literature as a whole is obtained. It is also very tedious for the author, who must check that the footnotes are correct. In other words, footnotes are better avoided.

Chronological method

With this commonly used method, authors are named in the text as required, using the surname (no initials) followed by the year of publication of the cited work in brackets ( ).

'This was first suggested by Brown (1934) who set in motion . . .'

Subsequent references to this work may use just the author's name unless another work by Brown (or another author with the same surname) is cited in the same part of the text and the two are likely to be confused. In the latter instance initials will have to be used. In the former case the year must be repeated each time. If this sort of confusion is going to occur frequently, then the numerical method described below should be preferred.

The references at the end of the chapter are arranged in alphabetical order of the authors' names. The year is given after the author's name as it was in the text, rather than in its usual place at the end of the reference. If this transposition of the date is not made, and there are several papers by one author, the reader has to check the end of the reference to make sure he or she has the correct one, which is somewhat irritating. There should be a subsidiary arrangement by date in such a case.

Confusion may occur if an author has published more than one paper in one year. In this case, the papers can be distinguished by using lower case letters immediately after the year – (1987a), (1987b), and so on. This obviously gives the subsidiary arrangement required in the list of references.

Numerical method

In many ways this is the system to be preferred as it is simpler to use, easy to check and there is no possibility of confusing similar references. The author is named in the text as before with a number in brackets immediately after.

'This was first suggested by Brown (2) in 1934 . . .'

The first work to be cited is given the number (1), the second (2) and so on to the end of the chapter. If a reference is cited more than once in the chapter then clearly its number remains the same. The numbered references are listed at the end of the chapter in the order in which they were cited. In the next chapter, the numbering starts at (1) again. In other words, each chapter is self-contained as regards the references.

As above, after the first citation of a work, subsequent mentions in that chapter need use only the author's name; however, if there is any likelihood of confusion with other works the number should also be used each time as this is a unique identification. In both the chronological and numerical methods it is clear that if any references are cited in more than one chapter then they will have to appear in more than one list of references. These two methods are widely used, especially in scientific and technical texts.

Ibid. and op. cit.

These two abbreviations cause untold trouble and confusion when used for citations and references, and are best avoided if there is any doubt as to their correct use. It is an old joke among librarians that students come with a book list complaining that they cannot find 'ibid.' in the catalogue, but it really does happen year after year. In most cases, neither of these abbreviations needs to be used as the information can be given in plain English. However, any extensive literature search, especially in the humanities, is likely to produce examples where they have been used so it does help to know what they mean.

Ibid. is short for the Latin word *ibidem* meaning 'in the same place'. In the text it is used to refer to a work or part of a work that has already been cited. This citation must be the last work that has been cited. If another work has been referred to between the original citation and the subsequent reference then ibid. may not be used. The use of the term is particularly common when literary works are referred to by name or when one work is being discussed chapter by chapter or line by line.

'Perhaps Mrs Gaskell's best known work is "*Cranford*" (1), which is the story of an old lady, Miss Matty, seen through the eyes of . . .'

A few lines later:

'Mrs Gaskell is also gifted at describing the village amusements such as the conjurer's visit (ibid. Chap. 9) . . .'

This is referring the reader to Chapter 9 of *Cranford*. As long as *Cranford* is the only work being discussed, ibid. may continue to be used. If at any time reference is made to any other work and the author then returns to a discussion of *Cranford*, then the work will have to be named properly once more.

Ibid. may also commonly be found in lists of references when the numerical system has been used in the text. For example:

1.   DICKENS, CHARLES, *Dickens's London*; essays selected and introduced by Rosalind Vailance. London, Folio Society, 1966.

2.   Ibid., pp. 31–36.
3.   Ibid., pp. 52–58.
4.   Ibid., pp. 84–87.

The reader is being referred to the different essays by this means.

If items nos. 6 and 7 were references to different works and no. 8 returned to part of *Dickens's London*, then either the full details would have to be given again, or, if no other work by Dickens features in the list of references, the following:

8.   DICKENS, CHARLES, op. cit., pp. 94–98.

This is saying that the work by Dickens that is referred to is the one already given in the list.

Op. cit. is another abbreviation from the Latin. It stands for *opere citato*, meaning 'in the work (already) quoted'. As has been shown above, the way it is used is very similar to ibid., but it is used when other works intervene between the original and the subsequent citation of a title.

When either of these abbreviations is used, it is important that there is not too long a gap between them and the original citation. It is most irritating to the reader to have to leaf back through several pages to work out what it is that is being referred to. It is particularly important, as in most methods of citation, not to carry over their use from one chapter to the next.

This system of citation is particularly useful when a single text is being analysed in some detail. However, it can be very tedious to check when the author is proof-reading. It is a system which does not have much current use, partly because all Latin terms and abbreviations are more rarely used, especially since the language is no longer widely taught in schools, and partly because it requires some extra care from the author.

Bibliography

In any work, in addition to the lists of references at the ends of each chapter, a complete bibliography should be constructed to insert at the end of the text. This should list all the items that appear in the various lists of references, together with any other material that has been used in the course of the project. The exception is unpublished material (other than theses) or material that is in preparation. In the former instances, if the reference is not generally available then there is little point in drawing it to the reader's attention. The appearance of the source 'personal communication' in a list of references is really no more than a sort of literary name-dropping. If personal communications have assisted the work in any substantial fashion, the person or persons involved may be included in the list of acknowledgements. In the latter instance, it may happen that such work is never published or is published in a drastically altered form. The reference could therefore be misleading. These remarks do not, of course, apply to manuscripts in archival collections that are properly documented.

Do not seek to impress by including all the results of the literature search. Some of these references will turn out to have only marginal relevance despite initially promising indications. Others will merely repeat information already obtained. These should be weeded out. A bibliography that contains everything, however remotely connected with the subject, merely indicates a lack of intelligent discrimination on the part of the author.

The bibliography should appear at the end of the main text, before any appendices. A brief note at the beginning should explain the principles on which the bibliography has been compiled. If the arrangement of the items is not perfectly obvious then this should be explained also. Most bibliographies for student theses or dissertations are best arranged either alphabetically by author's surname or chronologically by year of publication. This latter method should only be used when the date of the references is significant, for example if the project is tracing the development of a topic over a substantial period.

If the bibliography is very long indeed, neither of the above arrangements is particularly useful to the reader, who is forced to check through the entire list to make sure nothing of interest is overlooked. However, they have at least the merit of simplicity. As soon as more sophisticated arrangements are used, such as subject or format of publication, then other problems arise. For example, if arrangement under various subject headings is chosen, inevitably there will be material that would fit equally well under two or more headings or does not fit comfortably under any. This method can be very useful, though, as the reader interested in one particular aspect of the subject can quickly find the relevant material, and many topics fall naturally into discrete sections that can be reflected in the bibliography.

In historical works, it is common to find that the bibliography is divided into categories that reflect the type of source; for example, manuscripts, contemporary printed literature containing original material, contemporary journals and newspapers are all categories of primary sources. A further division for secondary printed material might also be included.

As a general rule, however, it is best to stick to a single sequence unless the number of items runs into the hundreds. If any other method is used there should be a convincing reason for it, and a careful explanation as to what has been done and why should be included in the introduction to the bibliography.

References

1. HART, C., *Doing a literature review; releasing the social science research imagination.* London, Sage, 1998, 230 pp.

2. BRITISH STANDARDS INSTITUTION, *Recommendations for citing and referencing published material.* Milton Keynes, B.S.I., 1990 (revised 1997) (BS 5605).

Index

SOCIAL SCIENCE LIBRARY
Oxford University Library Services
Manor Road
Oxford OX1 3UQ
Tel: (2)71093 (enquiries and renewals)
http://www.ssl.ox.ac.uk

This is a NORMAL LOAN item.

We will email you a reminder before this item is due.

Please see http://www.ssl.ox.ac.uk/lending.html
for details on:

- loan policies; these are also displayed on the notice boards and in our library guide.

- how to check when your books are due back.

- how to renew your books, including information on the maximum number of renewals.
  Items may be renewed if not reserved by another reader. Items must be renewed before the library closes on the due date.

- level of fines; fines are charged on overdue books.

Please note that this item may be recalled during Term.